I looked on child rearing not only as a work of
love and duty but as a profession that was fully
as interesting and challenging as any honourable
profession in the world and one that demanded
the best I could bring to it.

Rose Kennedy (1890-1995)

Play Around the Bay, Third Edition edited by Robin Bennett

Other Editing by A.K. Crump

First and Second Edition coauthored by Virginia Balogh-Rosenthal, Robin Bradley, Vickie Boudouris, Stefanie Eldred, Grace Fong, and Michelle O'Driscoll

Other Reviews & Submissions: Annette Achermann, Linda Burt, Pamela Canter, Caroline Cinti, Stephanie Green Crump, Angela Danison, Deborah DeLambert, Michelle Duffy, Lisa Evers, Maureen French, Diane Fried-laender, Hannah Goh, Carla Hashagen, Barbara Hurley, Joni Lachman, Edna Lee, Jennifer Lisi, Alexandra Matthews, Martha O'Connor, Sharon Ohlson, Sue Peipher, Lori Peltier, Carla Raddock, Lara Rajninger, Harriet Rosen, Susie Sorkin, Kathi Torres, Ellyn Weisel, Sonia Cehic, Frauke Bentzien, Mid-Peninsula Parents of Multiples

Cover Design: Heather McDonald (McDonald Design)
Layout Design: Robin Bennett

Photo Credits: Lisa Knutson Photography, TCB-Cafe Publishing, Members of the SFMOTC, Justin Sullivan (Lemurs), The Warren Family, the Bay Area Discovery Museum, San Francisco Zoological Society

Printing: DeHarts Printing, Santa Clara California

Many thanks are due to the Members and Board of the San Francisco Mothers of Twins Club (SFMOTC), Stacey Bolton, Elizabeth English, Paul Godwin (Music Together of SF)

tcb cafe publishing

PO Box 471706, San Francisco, CA 94147, www.cafeandre.com

ISBN   0-9674898-3-0

PLAY AROUND THE BAY:

A Guide to Bay Area Outings for Families with Young Children

*Connor and Jarryd negotiate the playground,
"Where to next? The swing, the slide, or the sandwich
in the diaper bag?""*

Table of Contents

North Bay
Sausalito, Tiburon, Mill Valley, San Rafael, Napa, etc.

Peninsula
San Mateo, Burlingame, Pacifica, Palo Alto, etc.

South Bay
San Jose, Cupertino, Sunnyvale, Los Gatos, etc.

Index

Foreword

From historical landmarks such as Angel Island, to art and science destination spots like the Bay Area Discovery Museum, the Bay Area sets the standard for active educational opportunities for children. Outings to the region's treasures allow children to learn and have fun at the same time. At the museums, zoos and parks all around the region, we bring families together to explore this extraordinary place that is the Bay Area.

Lori Fogarty, Executive Director
Bay Area Discovery Museum

Introduction

This book was quite a satisfying challenge. The challenge was to identify activities that children under the age of 5 and their caregivers might enjoy. The challenge was also due to the fact that children go through an incredible number of developmental stages between birth and turning 5, and their needs and abilities radically evolve from year to year, month to month...as do the needs of their parents. That is why we have asked parents of multiples, people who more than many others really need to get out of the house, to review activities around the San Francisco Bay and tell us from first-hand experience where they recommend you take children and why.

I would like to offer a big thank you to all those parents who took the time to contribute to this book. Those contributions often came after 10:00 PM, presumably after the kids were in bed, the dishes were done, bottles and/or food were prepared for the next day, the dog was walked and fed, and there were a few moments to breathe. It's quite an honor that these parents took those few minutes to share the jewels of the San Francisco Bay Area with other parents in need of recommendations. Whether your children are infants, toddlers, or preschoolers, single, doubles or triples, take this book in hand, pick a place, and get out of the house. I hope this book offers you new places with incredibly fun experiences.

Robin Bennett, Editor
3rd Edition, Play Around the Bay
San Francisco Mothers of Twins Club (SFMOTC)

About this Guide

Mothers of multiples know the importance of getting out of the house with kids! Where to go, however, is not as obvious. Although we found a few reference books on places to take kids in the Bay Area, none focus on the younger children or identify destinations that are easy to take more than one child. And NONE mention much about playgrounds - the destination visited most frequently by parents of young children.

This book does all that and more for San Francisco and the surrounding Bay Area. Each entry includes a brief description of an outing as well as general information on how to get there, how much it costs, when it's open, phone number and website address, and a suggested age range for which the activity is most appropriate. It also includes other information parents of young children want to know such as whether there is a bathroom, how easy is it to navigate a stroller, where to find food and snacks and how comfortable it is for one adult to manage with two or more young kids. The book is divided by geographic location into the following five sections: San Francisco, East Bay, North Bay, Peninsula, and South Bay. For each region, we list outings alphabetically within the following categories:

- **Playgrounds & Parks**
- **Animals: Zoos, Farms, & Nature Centers**
- **Museums: Art, Science and Hands-on** (that have exhibits geared toward young children)
- **Water Play: Beaches, Lakes, Pools & Boating** (places for young kids to swim or play in water)
- **Out and About: Hikes, Bikes & Stroller Walks** (paths that can accommodate young walkers as well as kids in backpacks or strollers)
- **More Outside Activities** (large outdoor areas where kids can run around and explore nature)
- **Amusements** (places that feature rides for toddlers or other amusements)
- **Trains, Planes & Automobiles** (train rides and transportation-related museums)

We tried to include as many fun outings as we could and still produce a book small enough to tuck into a car's glove compartment or diaper bag. Have fun!

San Francisco Mothers of Twins Club
http://sfmotc.org

The Bay Area is the perfect place to raise a cosmopolitan child and have a whole lot of fun doing it. You can take your future scientist to the Exploratorium in San Francisco, the Lawrence Hall of Science in Berkeley, or the Chabot Space & Science in Oakland. You and your young creative genius can wallow in arts and culture with world-class performances, museums, and festivals. Any child will enjoy the magic of the merry-go-round at Golden Gate Park or the thrill of building a sand castle on Stinson Beach in Marin County. Who cares whether or not your home has a yard? The whole Bay Area is your backyard and it offers a entire childhood's worth of inspiration, recreation, and good times.

Anne McSilver
Managing Editor, VIA magazine (AAA)

The Fragrance Garden in Golden Gate Park's Strybing Arboretum is a great place to take kids. In addition to the many wonderfully fragrant plants and flowers, it has a serene little pond with mossy rocks and tiny fish. There is a beautiful statue of St. Francis perfectly placed behind the pond with water quietly dripping from his hands. Once we even saw a bird standing on top of St. Francis' fingers.
This magical place is right next to a large field where my kids learned to play catch and frisbee. A short walk away is a large pond with turtles and many ducks. There are bathrooms close by and also Sunset area restaurants, stores and bus lines within several blocks.

David Harrington, founder of the Kronos Quartet

In San Francisco I walk my dog Bisou in Alta Plaza Park on Jackson Street. The park is high above the Bay, with a tremendous view from its children's playground that can't be beat.
A weekend favorite for a "chocolat chaud" is Crissy Field's Warming Hut in the Presidio, inside or outside at picnic tables if it's good weather. You can share the views of the Bridge with pelicans, early morning fishermen, joggers and friendly doggies.
Our school recently held its family picnic on Angel Island; everyone traveled by ferry from both sides of the Golden Gate Bridge for a sunny day playing pétanque, building sand chateaux on the little beach or hiking the trails around the island (bring your bicyclettes, no cars allowed).

Susie Shoaf
Lycée Français La Perouse
the International French School

The Exploratorium is one of most highly regarded science museums in the world. And it right in our own backyard. This is why San Francisco is a great place for visiting with kids, and for exploring outside the home. The exhibitry, programs, and structure of the Exploratorium develops that spark of intrigue, speculation, and questioning that is the very essence of learning.

Dr. Goery Delacote, Director
The Exploratorium

What makes the Randall Museum so much fun is that on any given day there are so many different things you can do. It's the only place in San Francisco, that I know of, where you can take a hike, throw a ceramic bowl, find out the magnitude of the most recent earthquake, watch a performance, do an art project, interact with live animals, AND have a picnic with your family enjoying amazing views of the City, all at the same place!

Nancy Ellis, Animal Exhibit Coordinator
Randall Museum

So many of us have come to the Bay Area from other parts of the country. Some of us, myself included, have even made the move from (gasp!) southern California. As a result, we may lack the social support system, as well as a knowledge of the City that would have come from being a 'local'. As a general pediatrician in San Francisco, I think it is wonderful when families help other families. The Mother of Twins group has a long history of just this type of support. With all the free time parents have, especially parents of twins (joke!), I'm sure I'll be overwhelmed by the sight of twins and singles at my next visit to the playground, park, or zoo. Congratulations and Enjoy!"

Alan Uba, MD
Associate Professor of Pediatrics
Division of General Pediatrics
University of California, San Francisco

Taking children to see and do new things on a regular basis is an important part of their development - it helps them learn about the world around them, and it gives parents more quality time with their family. The San Francisco Bay Area is a fantastic location for going out with kids. There are literally tons of outdoor activities available that are specifically tailored for children.

Michael Warren, Board Member
Pacific Primary School

Play Around the Bay Icons

Why Icons?

Based on feedback from the First & Second Editions of this guide, we have added a new system of icons for the most commonly asked questions parents have when preparing for an outing with their young children. These questions are not only due to convenience but also because of concerns for safety. For example, parents who are watching more than one small child are often relieved to find that the playground is enclosed by a fence, preventing a toddler from running into traffic or some other harm while the parent or caregiver is momentarily distracted.

These icons are also a fast and simple way to help you arrive at a decision on where to go and what to do today.

Icon Legend

 Parking provided or street parking available

 Bathrooms available during regular weekday hours

 Play area for young children is fenced and/or gated

Play area is single & double-stroller friendly

 Locale has structured programs for children 5 and under

 Access to play area may require going up a steep hill

Park may be cold, windy, or foggy at certain times of year

A child of five would understand this. Send somebody to fetch a child of five. -- Groucho Marx

San Francisco

There is a garden in every childhood, an enchanted place where colors are brighter, the air softer, and the morning more fragrant than ever again.

Elizabeth Lawrence

Parks & Playgrounds

Unless otherwise noted, San Francisco Recreation and Parks Department is the contact for information on the parks and playgrounds listed. The department can be reached at (415) 831–2700 or on the web at www.sfgov.org.

San Francisco

45th Avenue Playground

Golden Gate Park—45th Avenue/Lincoln Way

This playground is best for older toddlers but also offers early walkers some fun. It is located under a canopy of trees and possesses a wonderful wilderness feeling. A large wooden rowboat greets visitors to the park and gives the park its nickname—Boat Park. The boat easily holds and safely contains 30 children. There are two structures—one for older kids and one for toddlers. The structure

Let your little one set sail at Boat Park.

for toddlers includes two small double slides, while the other structure includes two long, high slides—one circular and one straight—that are both fun and dangerous for younger ones. Four infant swings and three regular swings round out the playground.

Other Activities   There are a few picnic tables in a grassy area adjacent to the playground. Plus, there are trails around the playground suitable for strollers. You can even hike over the hill to the beach.

Access   MUNI 18 46th Avenue, N Judah

Alta Plaza Park

Pacific Heights—Jackson Street/Steiner Street

This park has fabulous views of San Francisco and the Bay. The infant area is separated from the rest of the playground by a fence and includes a merry-go-round with carousel horses and a small wooden climbing structure with a wide slide. The whole area is a sandbox and plenty of benches allow parents to keep children in view. Three infant swings are located outside the infant area. There are four additional wooden/metal play structures, each progressively getting higher. The two smallest of the four are appropriate for the adventurous toddler. One includes a spiral slide, sliding pole, and metal net; and the other monkey bars and another sliding pole. Wooden paths cross the playground, meeting at a cement gazebo in the center of the playground. Unfortunately, these wooden paths are in the fall zones of most of the play structures.

(Playground renovations should begin summer of 2003.) Outside the fenced playground are tennis courts, a basketball court, and cement area for hopscotch and other games.

You can purchase food items on Fillmore Street or Divisadero Street.

MUNI 1 California, 3 Jackson, 12 Folsom-Pacific, 24 Divisadero

San Francisco

Bernal Heights Playground and Recreation Center

Bernal Heights—Moultrie Street/Jarboe Avenue
(415) 695–5007

This playground is appropriate for all age groups—crawlers through preschoolers, and includes three play structures, one of which is perfect for toddlers. There are plenty of swings, including a tire swing, and an open area below the park allows children to ride their push toys or ride a bike.

Bernal Heights Recreation Center offers Pee Wee Gym 10:00 a.m. to 12:00 p.m. every Tuesday and Thursday for children 18 months to 5 years.

Other Activities

You can get lunch along Cortland Street, have a picnic at the playground, and—after playing—head to the Bernal Heights branch of the San Francisco Public Library, located in front of the park.

Food

MUNI 24 Divisadero

Access

Blue Park

Golden Gate Park—10th Avenue/Fulton Street

The playground gets its name from the large, continuous blue play structure and is a favorite of many families. The structure includes a double slide, a wavy slide, and one spiral slide—all at a great height for older toddlers. It also includes monkey bars, a rope net ladder, two infant swings, and two regular swings. Sand and rubber matting underlie the play structure. The wonderful bridge that sits on the ground allows toddlers to safely run back and forth across it. This park has no fencing, although one side has a natural barrier of trees and shrubs. There is also a lot of open space for children to run around in. If your kids like to wander, you may find yourself running after them a lot.

The tunnel directly opposite the play structure leads to the California Academy of Sciences and the Japanese Tea Garden. The Strybing Arboretum & Botanical Gardens is just a bit farther. For little ones who like to keep moving, it is fun to start at the California Academy of Sciences and then go to the park or vice versa.

Other Activities

MUNI 5 Fulton, 21 Hayes, 31 Balboa, 44 O'Shaughnessy

Access

San Francisco

Children's Playground and Carousel

Golden Gate Park—3rd Avenue/Lincoln Way (Kezar)
(415) 753–5210

This playground is appropriate for all age groups—babies through preschoolers. It is very popular due to the variety of its play structures even though it is older and in need of some repair. The large play area has three distinct sections: an infant area with a play structure and slide that is separated from the toddler area by a walk-through tunnel; a toddler area with a wooden play structure, giant tire, and swings; and an area with a large wooden structure, circle swings, and a colorful honeycomb-shaped metal climbing structure that kids love to lose themselves in (parents cannot fit through this easily). There are long cement slides that the children slide down on pieces of cardboard, which is fun but not for the younger ones. The playground also includes a gymnastics area with rings, bars, and a horse. A beautifully restored turn-of-the-century carousel operates during summer months and weekends ($1 per adult and 25¢ per child), and a small snack bar is open on weekends. This is definitely a playground that requires two adults for two children.

Food Food can be picked up at any of the restaurants along upper Haight Street.

Other Activities Sharon Meadow, Conservatory of Flowers, Bocce ball courts, National AIDS Memorial Grove

Access MUNI 7 Haight, 33 Stanyan, 66 Quintara, 71 Haight-Noriega, N Judah

Chinese Playground

Chinatown—Sacramento Street/Waverly Place
(415) 274–0202

Celebrating over 75 years, Chinese Playground offers the toddler and older clean sand and a few structures not found in other playgrounds. The two separate play areas (underlain by sand and rubber cork) include a number of slides, a tire swing, a seesaw, rope climbing grid, spring-based pony rides, and a climbing wall. An interesting pulley-operated sand play structure lets kids scoop sand into big cups attached to a cable that they then hoist to dump down a tube. There is also a painted labyrinth and a large, colorful mural. Benches, but not tables, are found throughout the playground. An activity center includes four ping-pong tables and two tables for chess.

Food Food is available in nearby Chinatown. This is a perfect place to meet someone who works downtown for a brown bag lunch.

Access MUNI 1 California, 15 Third Street, 30 Stockton, 45 Union-Stockton, California Street Cable Car. Parking at the Portsmouth Garage or Sutter-Stockton Garage.

San Francisco

Christopher Playground

Diamond Heights—Diamond Heights Boulevard/Duncan Street
(415) 695–5000

This playground has two play areas with well-maintained wooden structures. The play area for older children is large and includes eight regular swings suspended from a dramatic archway and two large wooden structures with platforms and slides that rise to challenging heights. These are some of the largest play structures in San Francisco, so parents need to use their own judgment in allowing their children to play on them. At minimum, ambitious young climbers need extra supervision, especially if they attempt the curved, metal ladder-bridge that goes as high as 12 feet above the sandy ground.

The other play area has five infant swings and a climbing structure with slides, including a low one that is three-feet wide. There is also an intriguing, one-of-a-kind concrete structure that looks like Swiss cheese with plenty of holes for climbing. Surrounding this play area is a row of progressively lower wooden pilings that provide irresistible fun for good walkers, but watch out for the fall zones. A high fence separates the playground from a large grassy ball field that trainees from the Police Academy next door often jog around.

Food There is a grassy area for picnics adjacent to the playground, and provisions can be picked up at neighboring Diamond Heights Shopping Center.

Access MUNI 52 Excelsior. Two-hour parking is available in Diamond Heights Shopping Center.

Cow Hollow Playground

Cow Hollow—Miley Street (small street between Baker Street/Greenwich Street)
(415) 292–2003

This is a real gem of a playground. It is bi-level with stairs and a slide connecting the two areas. The upper level includes three infant swings, a wooden fort, a mini cable car—complete with bell, and a wide wooden walkway that provides a shaded crawl space for those in the lower level. The lower level includes a large play structure with monkey bars, rings, a spiral slide, and a metal tube. It is decorated with painted scenes of San Francisco landmarks. Both levels are above sand with a rubber pathway through the lower level. The lower level also includes three swings. There is plenty of space for

Jarryd rings the bell of a SF cable car.

San Francisco

children to play without interacting with the play structures, and both the play structures and the trees around the perimeter provide shade. The playground is fully fenced, and if your child should escape through one gate, they will be met by another gate at street level. The recreation center is quite active and very colorful with lots of light. This playground can be crowded, especially in the afternoons.

The recreation center hosts both a Toddler Group for those 9 months to 2 years 10:00 a.m. to 11:30 a.m. on Tuesdays and a Tiny Tots for those 2 years to 5 years 10:00 a.m. to 11:30 a.m. on Thursdays.

Food There isn't a grassy area in or around the playground, but there is one small picnic table. Food is available on nearby Union Street or Chestnut Street.

Access MUNI 41 Union, 45 Union-Stockton

Douglass Playground

Noe Valley—Douglass Street/26th Street
(415) 695–5017

This well-fenced park is ideal for all ages. It was recently renovated and now includes hard plastic/metal climbing structures—one suitable for younger toddlers and a more challenging one for older kids. It also includes two infant swings, two regular swings, and a stationary fire engine. These new additions, combined with a sand play area, a long metal slide built into the hill, basketball and tennis courts, and a large

Top: Spencer and Marisa make their way across the bridge.

grassy area bordered on one side by small cliffs and trees, make this a park that parents and children love. The accompanying recreation center provides top-notch services and play equipment. Younger children need supervision when they wander off near the hills and metal slide.

The recreation center offers two Tiny Tots programs. One is for those 3 to 5 and is held 10:00 a.m. to 12:00 p.m. every Tuesday. The other is for those 2 to 4 and is held 10:00 a.m. to 12:00 p.m. every Thursday. The recreation center also hosts a Toddler Drop-In for those 6 months to 2.5, held 10:00 a.m. to 12:00 p.m. every Friday.

Food Benches—a few shaded by trees—and picnic tables provide a good vantage point of most of the playground. Food is available at the Diamond Street Cafe (Diamond Street/24th Street) or at numerous spots along the nearby 24th Street commercial strip. Blackberry picking is great in the summer

Access MUNI 24 Divisadero leaves two steep blocks to climb; 35 Eureka eliminates all but one steep block, 48 24th Street, 52 Excelsior involves one long steep block

Duboce Park

Castro—Duboce Avenue/Scott Street

San Francisco

Designed and partly funded by Friends of Duboce Park, this new playground (April 2001) has colorful play structures not often found in other playgrounds. It includes a balance beam, climbing wall, and plastic lily pads that one can walk across. It also has the usual swings and a climbing structure with slides and overhead rings. The playground includes a sandbox and water fountain, as well as benches for sitting. The playground is adjacent to a huge grassy areas popular with neighborhood dog owners. In one corner of the park is the Harvey Milk Recreation Arts Center, which hosts Preschool Playdays for those 2.5 to 5. Playdays are held 10:00 a.m. to 11:30 a.m. Mondays, Wednesdays, and Fridays.

Food You can buy food a few blocks up Noe Street or down Duboce Avenue.

Access MUNI 22 Fillmore, 24 Divisadero, N Judah. Parking is available at CPMC (Davies Campus) Hospital.

Glen Park Playground and Recreation Center

Glen Park—Bosworth Street/O'Shaughnessy Boulevard
(415) 337-4705

This playground—appropriate for early walkers and preschoolers—includes a bi-level wooden play structure for climbing, long slides built into the hill, and swings for both infants and older children. The sand can be a bit dirty. There is a large grassy area—shared with dogs—with two baseball diamonds, tennis courts, and a recreation center with two gyms. A hiking trail and a stream behind the playground provide fun for preschoolers and older.

The recreation center hosts a variety of programs for children. Tiny Tots programs for those ages 3 to 5 is held 10:00 a.m. to 11:30 a.m. every Wednesday and Friday. There is also a Kids Gym program for those 1 to 2, held 10:00 a.m. to 11:30 a.m. every Tuesday and Thursday. Glen Park Recreation Center also hosts preschool field trips for those 1 to 5 every Monday 2:00 p.m. to 4:00 p.m.

Food The playground is a five-minute drive from Glen Park's main drag, Chenery Street, where you can find several eateries, a bookstore, and a bakery.

Access MUNI 44 O'Shaughnessy, BART Glen Park Station

San Francisco

Grattan Playground

Cole Valley—Alma Street/Stanyan Street
(415) 753-7039

This playground is best for the adventurous toddler and older, but is okay for early walkers. It is a bi-level playground with a wooden slatted bridge, tall tunnel and metal slides, and stairs and ramp connecting the two levels. The upper level includes three infant swings, a sandbox, and two wooden/metal climbing structures over sand. One structure is great for smaller children and includes a crawl tube. The second structure contains a wide slide, curved slide, tunnel, sliding pole, steering wheel, tubes, and ladders. Benches face the sandbox and climbing structures. The lower level has a great ring where you swing onto it and ride it across the sand. It also has very tall slides and sliding poles. Older kids tend to run through the younger kids' area so it is best for toddlers to visit during the morning. The park also has a large, gated grassy area, basketball courts, and tennis courts.

The recreation center hosts a Tiny Tots program for those ages 1 to 5, held 10:00 a.m. to 11:30 a.m. on Wednesdays.

Food   Food is located on nearby Cole Street.

Access   MUNI 6 Parnassus, 37 Corbett, 43 Masonic

Jackson Playground

Potrero Hill—17th Street/Carolina Street
(415) 554-9527

This playground is great for younger children. It is separated into two areas—one for babies and early walkers and one for preschoolers and older kids. A low wall—great for sitting and watching your children—separates the two areas and is decorated with hand-painted tiles. The baby area has a play structure, sandbox, seesaw, and picnic tables. The area for older children has two play structures—one with a fort and zipline—and swings. The park also has two baseball diamonds, a water fountain, tennis courts, and baseball and basketball courts. Note that school groups often crowd the play area during the week, so go early in the morning or on weekends. A new garden will be planted near the tennis courts during 2002/2003.

The recreation center hosts a Tiny Tots program for those ages 1 to 5, held 10:30 a.m. to 12:00 p.m. on Mondays, Wednesdays, and Saturdays.

Other Activities   There are a few picnic tables in the playground and restaurants are just a couple of blocks away at DeHaro Street and 16th Street.

The aroma of hops from Anchor Steam Brewery is sure to make

mouths water and the Basic Brown Bear Factory is one block away (see review on topic).
MUNI 10 Townsend, 19 Polk, 22 Fillmore

Julius Kahn Playground
The Presidio—Jackson Street/Spruce Street
(415) 292–2004

This playground is located in the Presidio among a grove of eucalyptus trees, and has two areas—one for toddlers and the other for older children. The playground is fenced (a very low fence that young children may be able to cross) with benches strategically placed throughout. The toddler structure includes two metal slides—one just a few feet off the ground, two sliding poles of different heights, and wide wooden boards connecting the different sides of the structure. The structure for older children contains one tall slide, one wavy slide, and one spiral slide, as well as large and small rings and monkey bars. These are older play structures and, as such, are quite high and some are in need of repair, i.e. splinters. The more adventurous child

Kate gets ready to fly on the slide.

may love them, but parents, of course, will need to judge what's appropriate for their child. This playground is best done with one adult per child.

Tennis courts, two baseball diamonds, and the recreation center are nearby. In addition, a hiking area where the trees are spaced widely apart can provide great wilderness opportunities.

There are some picnic tables outside. Food can be picked up from the Marina area—just a few minutes drive away.

Food

Junipero Serra Playground
Lakeside—Stonecrest Drive near Lyndhurst Drive
(415) 337–4713

This playground is great for crawlers to toddlers. Three infant swings, a tube structure with several cubby holes, and a small wooden/metal play structure provide wonderful play opportunities for the little ones. Parents can relax on several benches near the sand while keeping an eye on the entire playground. Toddlers can play on a structure that has a long, circular slide, and lots of overhead rings and bars. Plus, the kids

San Francisco

love to spin around and around on the two tire swings. A grassy area and baseball diamond are on a level lower than the playground. The tennis court and basketball court are adjacent to the playground.

Grab lunch at the Stonestown Galleria Shopping Center—just two blocks away—and visit the large children's section and fun aquariums at Border's Books.

The Merced branch of the San Francisco Public Library is just down the street and offers programs for toddlers and young children.

MUNI 17 Park Merced, 18 46th Avenue, 28 19th Avenue, 29 Sunset, M Ocean View

Laurel Hill Playground

Laurel Heights—Euclid Street/Collins Street
(415) 666–7007

This playground is appropriate for early walkers to preschoolers. The sand is really clean and the equipment is in good shape. The playground includes a wooden/metal play structure, spring-based pony ride-ons, slides, infant and regular swings, a baseball diamond, and tennis and basketball courts. The baseball diamond is reserved for children under the age of 12. Above the park is a concrete circle that is great for roller-skating or learning to ride a bike. The recreation center is well-stocked with lots of toys.

Other Activities One of the best things about the playground is the small room on-site that is home to the City College Child Observation Class. The facilitator has been teaching this class for ages and is very involved with the children. It is held 9:00 a.m. to noon and is open to those ages x to x.

The playground is located a few blocks from Laurel Village, an upscale shopping district with Imaginarium, GapKids, Starbucks, and fine eateries and delis.

Access MUNI 2 Clement

McCoppin Square

The Sunset—24th Avenue/Taraval Avenue

This playground is best suited for children 2.5 years and older, but is okay for crawlers and early walkers. It includes two wooden/metal play structures that sit on top of sand. There are four infant swings and four regular swings. A preschool and a couple of home day-care groups visit often, but the playground never seems crowded. Large, beautiful trees provide some shade and a pretty walkway leads to a grassy area with baseball diamonds. Sometimes a friendly police officer will stop by for a chat. Or, you can stop by the police station across the street and use their bathrooms and vending machines.

There is shopping on Taraval Street, including a produce market, cafe, restaurants, drugstore, and the Parkside brand of the San Francisco Public Library.

MUNI L Taraval

McKinley Square
Potrero Hill—Vermont Street/20th Street

This playground is great for crawlers, early walkers, preschoolers, and older. It was renovated in 2000 and has all new equipment. There are two play structures—one is very large, and six infant swings and an equal number of regular swings. An added bonus is that the swings are located at the far end of the park, reducing the risk that children will wander into the swing's path. There are eight slides with varying degrees of difficulty, two of which are perfect for even the smallest children. Kids will also enjoy playing on the two fun spring-based seesaw. The sand, as well as the whole

Sonja and Jakob work together.

park, is spotless. The play area is very large and completely fenced.

This playground sits high on Potrero Hill and offers stunning views. It can, however, get windy and cold in the afternoon. The large grassy area, which adjoins the park, is a favorite for dog owners and it can be fun for the children to safely watch the dogs run and play.

There are cafes and stores on Potrero Hill's main commercial strip just **Food** a short drive (or very hilly walk) away. San Francisco's second most crookedest street—Vermont Street—is nearby.

MUNI 19 Polk (steep walk uphill to playground), 53 Southern Heights   **Access**

Midtown Terrace Playground
Midtown Terrace—Clarendon Avenue/Olympia Way
(415) 753-7036

This is a gem of a playground. The fenced area includes everything behind the recreation center—play structures, large grassy field, gardens and trees on a hill, and another set of play structures on the other side of the

San Francisco

grassy area. There are two wooden/metal play structure underlain by sand that will entertain and delight toddlers—crawlers and early walkers will have a more difficult time. One structure, for older kids, includes a tall metal slide, sliding pole, and rings. The structure for younger children includes a short, wide slide, metal tube, and a steering wheel on the highest level. The play area, however, is interesting for children of all ages and includes a tire swing, three infant swings, a large merry-go-round, and two metal spring-based structures. Across the grassy field is another play area for older children, but it is underlain by grass. There's also a generous paved area that is a safe place for younger children to ride their bikes or use push toys.

Zoe loves the swings.

A fire station across the street welcomes young visitors. The recreation center offers a variety of programs for children of all age, including a PeeWee Playday for those 2.5 to 5 years at 10:00 a.m. to 11:30 a.m. Tuesdays and Thursdays.

Access MUNI 36 Teresita

Miraloma Playground

Miraloma Park—Omar/Sequoia Ways
(415) 337–4704

This well-kept secret of a playground—appropriate for crawlers, early walkers, and toddlers—has fabulous views and is very clean. It includes two play areas separated by two rows of bushes and a concrete sidewalk. Numerous benches, allowing parents to easily keep an eye on their younger children, surround the smaller play area. It includes three infant swings, a wooden/metal play structure with bridge and short slide, and balance beams and posts just inches above the sand base. This allows crawlers and early walkers plenty of challenges. The wooden/metal play structure in the larger area has lots of rings, a long, circular slide, and a tall metal slide, and four regular swings.

Other Activities The playground area is well-fenced with a gate to the grassy area and baseball diamonds on the lower level. Basketball and tennis courts are in good shape. The park is rarely frequented by groups. However, the park does get cold and windy in the summer months.

Food Restaurants and markets are on Portola Drive—several steep blocks away.

Access MUNI 36 Teresita

Mission Dolores Park

The Mission—Dolores Street/18th Street
(415) 554-5008

San Francisco

Located a few blocks from historic Mission Dolores, this playground offers wonderful views of San Francisco's downtown area. The playground is appropriate for preschoolers and older children and is on a small plateau with climbing structures, a sand area, metal slides, swings, monkey bars, a covered boat,   and hopscotch courts. Older toddlers (upwards of 2.5) love the wooden climbing structures that pose a more challenging alternative to the newer—and safer—hard plastic ones. Younger kids, however, will find most structures too high to climb without help. The area surrounding the play structures is sloped and hence very frustrating for early walkers.

The playground area is not fenced, but is surrounded by a grassy area that discourages kids from running off. It gets some school groups during the week, lots of families on sunny weekends, and occasionally kids between classes from Mission High, but it is rarely crowded. The park also has tennis and basketball courts and a grassy area popular with dogs.

Food is available at nearby Dolores Park Cafe (18th and Dolores Street) or from Bi-Rite Market (18th between Dolores and Guerrero streets).

Food

MUNI 33 Stanyan, J Church

Access

Mission Playground

The Mission—Valencia Street/Cunningham
(415) 695-5008

This hidden oasis with clean sand, terrific play structures, and a landscaped sitting area that affords a good view of the whole playground is appropriate for all ages. The playground was revamped a few years ago and now has Landscape Structures brand equipment, including a climbing and sliding structure for younger kids, as well as a more extensive one for older kids. It also includes two infant swings, four regular swings, one tire swing, three spring-based rocking horses, and a large train structure that kids of all ages enjoy playing in or climbing on.

The location offers some of the best weather in the city and the kids' playground is blocked by wind from the adjoining recreation center. In really sunny weather, the only shade is in the sand under the play structures or in the recreation center. The complex also has tennis and basketball courts as well as an asphalt ball park and walled-in outdoor pool. The pool has undergone a renovation of its locker rooms and the addition of a ramp. Call the recreation center about the Spanish Bilingual Tiny Tots program.

San Francisco

Food is available at the nearby Dolores Park Cafe (18th and Dolores Street) or from Bi-Rite Market (18th between Dolores and Guerrero streets) or numerous other spots on the popular Valencia corridor. However, there really isn't any place at the playground for a picnic.

MUNI 14 Mission, 26 Valencia, 33 Stanyan, 49 Van Ness/Mission

Mountain Lake Park

The Presidio—12th Avenue/Lake Street

This is a nice playground for stroller walks as there is a path around one side of the lake. This bi-level playground is most appropriate for preschoolers and older children. For 3- to 5-year-olds, there is a cement slide from one level down to the other and a high climbing structure. Although, some less adventurous children (and parents) might find it a bit too high. There is one small slide for toddlers and another slide made from rollers. There are quite a few regular swings and four infant swings. The sand is relatively clean and there is a great grassy area. The duck pond is a plus, but because seagulls and pigeons also have taken up residence, the pond area can be pretty dirty. Children still love to feed the ducks in the lake.

There are short hikes beyond the lakes that are good for double joggers and those with dogs.

Access MUNI 1 California, 28 19th Avenue

JP Murphy Playground

Inner Sunset—9th Ave between Ortega and Pacheco Streets
(415) 753-7099

This playground is ideal for older toddlers. Wooden and metal play structures sit on top of sand. There's a metal climbing structure that resembles a gazebo and a large swinging bridge that challenges and amuses older children. There are infant swings, as well as regular swings. The park also includes a basketball court, three tennis courts, and a hopscotch area.

Other Activities The recreation center offers a Junior Tiny Tots for those 2 to 4 held 10:30 a.m. to 12:00 p.m. Wednesdays and a Tiny Tots program for those 3.5 to 5 held 10:30 a.m. to 12:00 p.m. on Tuesdays. There is also a Kids Gym for those 1 to 5, held 10:30 a.m. to 11:30 a.m. on Thursdays.

Access MUNI 6 Parnassus

Noe Valley Courts
Noe Valley—Douglass Street between 24th Street /Elizabeth Street

San Francisco

This is a very small playground with a very small play structure that is perfect for very young kids. It has the only slide that crawlers can successfully navigate by themselves! The playground also has one tire swing, one toddler swing, and one infant swing. Toddlers and older kids use the park's tennis and basketball courts for ball play and bike riding. The small setting is very conducive for talking to the occasional other mom or the many nannies found during the week before 5:00 p.m.. Active older toddlers can learn how to get around the gate separating the playground from the street, so the park looses its luster for caregivers with more than one older child. The grassy area serves as a popular dog run and is separated from the children's playground by a small wall—problems occasionally surface in the form of dog waste on the grass or by a dog straying into children's area. The park gets crowded after 2:30 p.m. when nearby Alvarado School lets out. Strollers are left on the sidewalk outside the gate or in the grassy area close to the playground.

Food Food is available at Diamond Street Cafe (Diamond and 24th streets) or at numerous spots along the nearby 24th Street commercial strip.

Access MUNI 48 24th Street

Moscone Playground & Recreation Center
The Marina—Chestnut Street/Buchanan
(415) 292–2006

This is a beautiful, brand new playground appropriate for all ages—crawlers to older children. It is well-fenced and includes two wooden/metal climbing structures for older children and a small climbing structure for early walkers and toddlers. There are three baby swings but no swings for older children. An enclosed, fort-like area and a loft area are great for imaginative play.

The main drawback - it is always mobbed. While it is definitely doable by one parent with two kids because it is so well enclosed, it is easy to loose sight of a child because there are just SO many people there.

Picnic tables are located in the playground. And, food can be found at nearby restaurants on Chestnut and Union Streets.

Other Activities A large recreation center with programs for all ages is on one side of the playground and a library is on the other. The library also offers programs for children of different ages. The recreation center offers a Kids Gym for those nine months to 36 months 10:00 a.m. to 12:00 p.m. Thursdays and Fridays, as well as two Tiny Tots program. One is from

San Francisco

those two and half to three and a half years-old 10:00 a.m. to 12:00 p.m. Tuesdays. The other is for those three to five years old 10:00 a.m. to 12:00 p.m. Wednesdays.

Food is available nearby on Chestnut Street.

MUNI 28 19th Avenue, 30 Stockton, 22 Fillmore, 43 Masonic

North Beach Playground
North Beach—Lombard Street/Mason Street
(415) 274-0201

For those who find themselves in North Beach with kids who need to run off a little energy, North Beach Playground offers a better alternative than the Washington Square playground. The playground is separated by fence into two areas—one for older children and one for toddlers and younger. The younger area includes a small wooden structure with steps and climbing blocks and a wide slide. There are also two rocking horses and water fountain. The area provides some shade and lots of benches for parents to watch their children. The older kids' area has four wooden and metal play structures—some of them in need of repair. There are numerous slides, lots of stepping blocks, infant and regular swings, and monkey bars. There is also a structure made of wooden balance beams at varying heights and angles that can provide children with great challenges.

Food Grab lunch anywhere along Columbus Avenue. Although there are picnic tables at the playground, they are in varying states of repair.

The North Beach branch of the San Francisco Public Library is adjacent to the playground.

Access MUNI 15 Third Street, 30 Stockton, 39 Coit

Pacific Bell Park's Coca-Cola Fan Lot
China Basin—3rd Street/King Street
(415) 972-2000 / www.sfgiants.com

Hours: September to May—11:00 a.m. to 5:00 p.m. Thursday through Sunday; June to August—11:00 a.m. to 5:00 p.m. daily except on game days

Pacific Bell Park's Coca-Cola Fan Lot is free and open to the public. Attractions include the Coca-Cola Superslide, a Little Giants Park, a Base Race, and the baseball glove easily seen from the street. Children who are at least 20" tall will enjoy the two 20' long twisting slides appropriately named Twist Off, while those who are at least 42" tall will be challenged with the two 56' long curving slides named Guzzler. The

Little Giants Park—a junior-sized replica of PacBell Park for children ages 3 to 7—includes a baseball diamond where batters take turns hitting a pitched whiffle ball and then running around the bases. Three different bat sizes are available and staff give pointers on technique. The Pitcher Challenge allows kids to take turns throwing balls against pictures of a catcher and a batter.

The concession stands are not open at PacBell Park on non-game days. Cafes are along The Embarcadero.

Tours of PacBell Park are available daily from 10:00 a.m. to 2:00 p.m. on non-game days. The tour covers approximately two miles in 75 minutes is $10 for adults and $5 for children 12 and under. The area also includes a fishing pier that offers great views of boats, the Bay Bridge, and the East Bay. A fence separates the walkway from the water, but you'll have to keep close watch on wandering toddlers as it might be possible for the really determined to squeeze through. A bit further down on Herb Caen Way, you'll find the new South Beach Children's Play Area (see review on topic).

Access MUNI 10 Townsend, 30 Stockton, 45 Union-Stockton, 76 Marin Headlands, N Judah, Caltrain. Enter the Coca-Cola Fan Lot via the stairs or elevator to the left of the Marine Gate near the seal statue and the China Basin Ferry Terminal

San Francisco

Panhandle Playground
Golden Gate Park—Ashbury Street/Oak Street
(415) 554–9530

This is an excellent playground for crawlers, early walkers, toddlers, and preschoolers. A new play structure—Kids Kingdom—dominates the playground and provides numerous shaded cubby areas under the

structure, as well as many fun little huts to climb in and through. It also contains a rope for climbing and footholds to help the smaller climber. A small, curved sliding pole allows the youngest toddlers to slowly make their way to the ground. Wooden pathways lead from the cement perimeter where the benches and picnic tables are located, over the sand and to the play structure. The playground also includes one tire swing over rubber matting, two infant swings, and two older swings. The climbing structure is the perfect height for smaller children. Eucalyptus trees provide shade for the park. The park is completely fenced and you can see almost every part of it from

Jarryd and Spencer ride the train, while Marissa and Matthew swing the tire.

San Francisco

the benches, so it is perfect for young twins. There is a trail that runs right by it.

Haight Street is just a few blocks away with plenty of places to eat and shop. There are two picnic tables within the fenced playground and plenty of grassy areas outside the playground.

MUNI 33 Stanyan, 43 Masonic

Parkside Square
The Sunset—26th Avenue/Vicente

This playground is best for adventurous toddlers and older. There are two wooden/metal play structures sitting on top of sand, as well as a merry-go-round, three infant swings, eight swings for older children, and three slides of varying heights. The playground is partly fenced and, although you must cross a large field to get to the street, the parking lot is only a few steps away. A basketball court and tennis courts are located nearby.

Food
There are picnic tables near the playground and snacks can be found two blocks away on Taraval Street.

The park borders Stern Grove, a wooded area with trails that is the site of a fabulous concert series on Sundays during the summer.

Access
MUNI 66 Quintara, L Taraval

Peixotto Playground
Buena Vista—15th Street near Roosevelt

Because it is not visible from the street (and the sign for the co-op leads you to wonder whether it is on private property), this playground is a hidden gem—especially on weekends when the nursery school is closed. The San Francisco Recreation and Parks Department manages the playground so it can be used even when the nursery school is in session. It is bordered on one side by the cliffs of the Corona Heights mountain, home of the Randall Museum. The playground is most appropriate for those over the age of 3. There is a single, older (though well-maintained) wooden and metal play structure over sand that graduates in height to 7 feet, so you have to watch that younger toddlers don't venture up past their (or your) comfort zone. There isn't a separate sand pit, so crawlers aren't protected from older kids. Besides swings (infant and toddler) and the climbing structure that includes ladders, a wooden bridge, tunnel, small slide, large 7-foot metal slide, 7-foot curved slide, and a sliding pole, there is a small merry-go-round and working water fountain that can actually be reached by younger kids. The playground is not gated on all sides. There is an open entrance leading to Beaver Street. There are benches at the playground but no picnic tables. Food can be purchased from delis on Divisadero Street.

Randall Museum is nearby.

MUNI 24 Divisadero

San Francisco

Presidio Heights Playground

Presidio Heights—Clay Street between Laurel/Walnut Streets
(415) 295-2005

This is a small playground with older wooden and metal play structures. It is best suited for toddlers and preschoolers. One wooden/metal structure includes a metal net ladder, small rings, and narrow metal slide. An older, metal octagon structure contains swinging bars, rings, and ladders that criss-cross the top of the tall structure. Be sure to watch your children carefully if you allow them to play on this structure. The play area includes concrete basketball courts and a tennis court.

The recreation center offers a Toddler Play Group for those under 2 years 10:00 a.m. to 11:30 a.m. Mondays, and a Tiny Tots program for those 3 to 5 years 10:00 a.m. to 12:00 p.m. Fridays.

Food and shops can be found just a block away around the Sacramento and Presidio streets area.

Food

MUNI 1 California, 3 Jackson, 4 Sutter, 43 Masonic

Access

South Beach Children's Play Area

China Basin—King Street/The Embarcadero

An urban design and landscape architect firm, with lots of community input, built South Beach Park's new Children's Play Area. The nautical-themed playground features a low wave wall, a net grid climbing structure, a sandbox with a tugboat, a couple of spring-based ride-on toys, and a merry-go-round. This playground is underlain by rubber matting and is designed for children under 5 years of age. The sandbox is on the sidelines, allowing parents of crawlers and early walkers to keep their children from eating fistfuls of sand! Plus, the crawlers and early walkers will love climbing over and around the wave wall.

Grab a lunch at any of the cafes nearby or bring a sack lunch to the playground, which has benches and picnic tables.

Make it a playground day and head over to Pacific Bell Park's Coca-Cola Fan Lot. Or, take a long stroller walk along The Embarcadero.

Other Activities

MUNI 10 Townsend, N Judah. Parking is plentiful (except on Game Days) on the Bay side of The Embarcadero at the intersection of Townsend Street.

Access

San Francisco

Sunset Playground and Recreation Center
The Sunset—28th Avenue/Lawton Street
(415) 753-7098

This playground includes two wooden play areas, one for toddlers and one for older children. A sandbox and a few infant swings are in the toddler area, while regular swings and a merry-go-round are in the area for older children. The recreation center houses a large gym with ping pong tables, basketball courts, and an auditorium. The park also includes a tennis court and a baseball diamond. Sometimes, it gets crowded during the school year.

Activities The recreation center hosts a variety of programs including a Kids Gym for those 1 to 2 years 10:30 a.m. to 12:00 p.m. Wednesdays and 10:00 a.m. to 11:30 a.m. Thursdays. It also holds a Mom's & Tots program for those 1 to 5 11:30 a.m. to 1:00 p.m. Tuesdays; a Tiny Tots program for those 3 to 5 10:30 a.m. to 12:00 p.m. Mondays and Fridays, and a Pee Wee Sports for those 4 and 5 1:30 p.m. to 2:30 p.m. Thursdays.

Access MUNI 71 Haight-Noriega, N Judah

Upper Noe Playground and Recreation Center
Noe Valley—Day/Sanchez Streets
(415) 695-5011

This is a well-gated facility with an aging wooden and metal play structure that good climbers love. It includes ramps, ladders, steps made of wood pilings, wooden bridge, slides, wooden caves, and enough space under the structure to provide a shady place to play. There is also a curved metal climbing grid, four older kid swings, and four infant swings, as well as a sandpit for younger children. The entire playground is covered in sand. Benches are located close to the sandpit (a few in the shade) and across from the play structure. The playground is okay for kids of all ages, but most appropriate for those 2 and older. The playground can be accessed via a ramp from Day Street near the corner of Sanchez Street.

Activities The recreation center offers a the widest variety of programs for children from 12 months to 5 years than any other playground in San Francisco. Offerings include Tiny Tots and Kids Gym. Many programs are free. The park includes a gymnasium, tennis courts, basketball courts, and baseball field. The gym can get crowded on rainy days.

Food Food is available a block away on Church Street.

Access MUNI 24 Divisadero, J Church

West Portal Playground
West Portal—Ulloa Street/Lenox Way
(415) 753–7038

This playground has one large play structure with swinging bridges, a sliding pole, little slides, and larger slides. There is also a train structure that's excellent for crawlers and early walkers. The play structure sits on sand and the swings are on soft tarmac. There's an area for playing four-square and hopscotch and a large grassy area that is adjacent to the playground and well-fenced. Dogs share the grassy area but leave it clean. It tends to be crowded during the week because of the school next door.

The recreation center offers a Tiny Tots program for those 1 to 4 years 10:00 a.m. to 11:30 a.m. Mondays and for 2- and 3-year-olds 10:30 a.m. to 12:00 p.m. Wednesdays.

Food

Shopping (markets, drugstores, restaurants, toy stores, bookstore, movie theatre) is within easy walking distance. The West Portal branch of the San Francisco Public Library is nearby, and has an excellent children's section, and offers a lapsit program for all ages throughout the week.

Activities

MUNI 48 Qunitara-24th Street, K Ingleside, L Taraval, M Ocean View

Access

West Sunset Playground
The Sunset—39th Avenue/Ortega
(415) 753–7047

This large playground is best suited for older toddlers and above, but there are play items for younger children. One wooden/metal play structure is very tall and includes a long metal slide and sliding pole. It also includes monkey bars, large rings, and small rings. A smaller wooden/metal structure includes two short, wide slides and one longer slide. The playground includes an enclosed sand pit for young crawlers and early walkers, three infant swings, and six other swings. The playground is only partially fenced but the street is a safe distance away. A middle school, a recreation center, and a public library encircle the playground. There are tennis courts on one side of the playground and a grassy field with baseball diamonds on the other side of the tennis courts. There is a paved, unfenced area on the other side of the playground studded by trees and benches. Middle school children use the playground during the day.

MUNI 29 Sunset, 48 24th Street

Access

Animals: Zoos, Farms, & Nature Centers

San Francisco

Aquarium of the Bay

Pier 39—The Embarcadero/Beach Street
(888) SEA–DIVE / www.aquariumofthebay.com

Hours: Open daily 10:00 a.m. to 6:00 p.m. Monday through Friday
10:00 a.m. to 7:00 p.m. Saturday through Sunday
Summer — 9:00 a.m. to 8:00 p.m.
Closed December 25.

Fees: Adults (12–64) $12.95, Children (3–11) / Seniors (65+) $6.50
Family $29.95 for two adults and two children. Family Membership $65

Aquarium of the Bay offers an extraordinary underwater adventure. Two 300-feet-long transparent tunnels provide an amazing view of the marine life of the San Francisco Bay. Kids will love getting up close and personal with fish, sharks, eels, bat rays, and other sea creatures that swim by. And, there are plenty of staff naturalists ready to answer questions. The highlight for kids older than 4, however, is the chance to pet the sharks! Three petting tanks are found at the end of the exhibit, one containing bat rays, one containing starfish, and one containing leopard sharks and two other shark species. The delight of petting the sharks is well worth the entrance fee!

Food There are plenty of eateries to choose from on Pier 39 or nearby Fisherman's Wharf.

Activities Pier 39 (see review) has plenty of other attractions including a two-tiered Venetian carousel and a chance to watch sea lions sun themselves on floats west of the pier.

Access MUNI 10 Townsend, 15 Third Street, 39 COIT, 47 Van Ness, F Market & Wharves historic streetcar

Randall Museum

Buena Vista—199 Museum Way
(415) 554–9600 / www.randallmuseum.org

San Francisco

Hours: 10:00 a.m. to 5:00 p.m. Tuesday through Saturday
Closed national holidays.

Fees: Entrance is free. There is a fee for the classes.

The Randall Museum is dedicated to education and the environment and offers many classes and performances. Saturdays include drop-in workshops from 1:00 p.m. to 4:00 p.m., including a family ceramics workshop from 10:00 a.m. to 11:15 a.m. for ages 3 and up; a terrific room-sized railroad model exhibit sponsored by the Golden Gate Model Railroad Club 11:00 a.m. to 4:00 p.m.; Meet the Animals 11:15 a.m. to 12:00 p.m., and animal feedings 12:00 p.m. in addition to special exhibits such as Giant Puppets, Bug Day, and the annual July Butterfly count.

The Randall Museum is expected to complete construction of its Outdoor Plan 2002/2003. Once construction is completed, planting will begin for the many child-friendly educational gardens planned: the flower garden, an herb garden, a lemon garden, a lime garden, a mushroom garden, a dinosaur garden featuring a collection of primitive living fossil trees and other ancient plants that have existed since the time of dinosaurs, an animal exhibit garden, a tropical garden, a cactulent garden, and the Hummerbumblebutterbee Rock Garden.

Activities

The hiking behind the museum offers gorgeous views of the city. You can also try Pexiotto Playground at Beaver Street and 15th (see review) Street.

Access

MUNI 37 Corbett

San Francisco

San Francisco Zoo

The Sunset—1 Zoo Road (45th Avenue/Sloat Boulevard)
(415) 753-7080 / www.sfzoo.org

Hours: 10:00 a.m. to 5:00 p.m. Daily
Children's Zoo opens at 11:00 a.m.

Fees: San Francisco Residents—Adults (18-64) $8, Youths (12-17) / Seniors (65+):
$3.50, Children (3-11) $1.50; Family Membership: $65. Non-San Francisco residents pay slightly more. Free first Wednesday of the month.. Parking is free
except the main lot at the Front Gate, which is $4.00

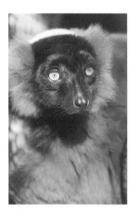

Preschoolers will love interacting with the exhibits in the newly opened Lipman Family Lemur Forest, the largest outdoor multi-species lemur habitat in the country. Plus, all ages will enjoy the new, expanded Children's Zoo that includes barnyard animal feedings at the Family Farm, an insect zoo, bunnies, a prairie dog/meerkat exhibit, and a nature walk featuring teenage docents with live animals during the summer months. Other attractions at the zoo include penguin island, the big cat feeding at 2:00 p.m., gorilla world, Puente al Sur (South American animals), the peaceful feline conservation center, and the ever-popular carousel that was restored in 2002 ($2 for two rides; adults ride free with children). The Little Puffer steam train (see description elsewhere) is a must-do for children ($2 for all over age 3).

The playground, next to a large grassy field with shade trees, has three play structures (one with a large tube tunnel slide), swings, and two other play areas for early walkers. The zoo is a great activity for parents with stroller-bound children. Enjoy a walk around the zoo, pointing out the animal noises and smells and then picnic near the playground or in the Children's Zoo area.

Activities The new education center offers numerous classes for children age 3 and older. Plus, families can camp out at the zoo and enjoy a night safari. See the zoo's web site for a current schedule. Wagons and carts can be rented near the zoo entrance. The gift shop is a fun stop with many inexpensive items. Family membership to the zoo is a worthwhile purchase and allows entrance to Happy Hollow Zoo in San Jose and the Oakland Zoo, as well as zoos around the country.

Food There are several cafes at the zoo that serve the basics—hamburgers, hot dogs, veggie burgers, Gordon Biersch garlic fries, etc.

Access MUNI 18 46th Ave., 23 Monterey, L Taraval

Museums: Art, Science, & Hands-On

California Academy of Sciences
Golden Gate Park—55 Concourse Drive
(415) 750-7145 / www.calacademy.org

San Francisco

Hours: Labor Day to Memorial Day — 10:00 a.m. to 5:00 p.m.
Memorial Day to Labor Day — 9:00 a.m. to 6:00 p.m.

Fees: Adults (18–64) $8.50, Youth (12–17) / Students / Seniors (65+)
$5.50, Children (4–11) $2.00, Under 4 free. Family Membership: $60.
Free first Wednesday of the month.

This should be called the "California Academy of Toddlers" as those seem to be it's main patrons. The African Hall and Native California Hall offer dioramas full of lions and tigers and bears. This is a great place to go on a cold or rainy weekday. It is almost never crowded—except on the cold and rainy days—and crawlers to toddlers can roam free due to the huge halls and thus endless line of sight. There is also a nice little toddler play area at the far end of the African Hall that has puzzles, puppets, books, and interactive games. This area is wonderful until your children learn how to push the small swing doors and escape. The Aquarium is better visited with two adults (or with children who don't mind staying in their strollers). It is dark in most places and children can easily get lost or jostled by unsuspecting aquarium visitors.

Food The cafe is not too overly priced and is well stocked with kid-friendly food items and high chairs. Museum members receive a 10% discount.

Activities The Academy is across from the Japanese Tea Garden and around the corner from the Strybing Arboretum. It's also just a short walk from Blue Park and Sharon Meadow, as well as the 9th and Irving neighborhood, good for shopping and food.

Access MUNI 5 Fulton, 44 O'Shaughnessy

San Francisco

Exploratorium

The Marina—3601 Lyon St.
(415) EXP.LORE / www.exploratorium.edu

Hours: Memorial Day to Labor Day—10:00 a.m. to 6:00 p.m. Tuesday through Sunday,
10:00 a.m. to 9:00 p.m. Wednesday
Labor Day to Memorial Day—10:00 a.m. to 5:00 p.m. Tuesday through Sunday
10:00 a.m. to 9:00 p.m., Wednesday
Closed Mondays, Thanksgiving, and Christmas

Fees: Adults (18–64) $10.00, Seniors (65+) $7.50, Youth (5-17) $6.00, Children (0–4)
and Members free. Tactile Dome $14,00, includes admission. First Wednesday
of month is free.

A hands-on museum with over 650 interactive exhibits, experiences, and experiments. You can catch shadows, turn knobs, speak into a gigantic echo tube, blow bubbles, view an active geyser, watch yourself "fly" and make rainbows, just to list a few of the available activities. All the senses are tickled as you explore light, color, vision, electricity and magnetism, life sciences, heat and temperature, sound, vibrations, speech and hearing and complexity. There is also an enclosed interactive area for young toddlers (Playlab) with books, toys, magnets, instruments and knobs. The vastness of the Exploratorium can be a little overwhelming so trying to see just one part of the museum can be more rewarding. This museum tends to be quite crowded with school groups, so the best time to visit is after 2:00 p.m. or during the months of August/September.

Although Exploratorium is entertaining, it is over the heads of kids under 3. While the 3- to 5-year-old set is probably too young to understand most of the exhibits, it is still fun for them to interact with the exhibits. It is relatively dark inside, so it can be difficult to keep track of two small children. This is definitely a one adult per child activity.

Food   You can have a snack or lunch at the cafe inside the Exploratorium, or visit the coffee cart at the entrance.

Activities   Don't forget to leave some time for a walk at the Palace of Fine Arts. The adjacent duck pond is fenced.

Access   MUNI 22 Fillmore, 28 19th Avenue, 30 Stockton, 41 Union, 43 Masonic, 45 Union-Stockton

Water Play: Beaches, Lakes, Pools, & Boating

San Francisco

Aquatic Park

Fisherman's Wharf—Beach Street between Van Ness/Hyde Streets

Aquatic Park, a small beach with viewing stands and promenade encircled by the Municipal Pier and the Hyde Street Pier, is a welcome respite from the commercial chaos of nearby Fisherman's Wharf. It offers terrific views of Alcatraz, the Golden Gate Bridge, and the ships of Hyde Street Pier as well as the occasional hearty soul out for a swim in the frigid waters of the Bay. The promenade is great for walking with or without a stroller. The beach is fine for kids who want to play in the sand. Be wary of broken glass.

Food
A nearby grassy area is great for a picnic. Pick up lunch at any one of the eateries in the neighborhood.

Activities
Walk from the National Maritime Museum to Hyde Street Pier via the wonderful Aquatic Park beach and promenade (see review). Or, extend your walk to Fort Point (see review). This activity is within walking distance of the shops, eateries, and amusements of Fisherman's Wharf, The Cannery, and Ghiradelli Square. You can also watch fishing off the Municipal Pier. Crafts people often set up on nearby Beach Street.

Access
MUNI 19 Polk, 47 Van Ness, 49 Van Ness-Mission, F Market & Wharves historic streetcar, Powell-Hyde Cable Car

Baker Beach

The Presidio—Lincoln Boulevard
(415) 561-4323

A favorite destination of many parents, Baker Beach offers panoramic views of the Pacific side of the Golden Gate Bridge and the Marin headlands. Besides the view, you can watch shipping traffic going in and out of the Golden Gate, seals playing in the water, or fishermen working their lines in the morning. The beach and parking area are virtually empty before 10:00 a.m., but get busy by noon. Although the water is cold and the Pacific waters uncertain (children should always be hand-held), there's lots of great sand for digging. Be sure to bring sweaters/long pants in case it's windy or cold.

Food
Baker Beach has sheltered picnic tables and grills, so bring a picnic with you. There isn't any food nearby.

Access
MUNI 29 Sunset. If driving, enter Baker Beach from Lincoln Boulevard in the Presidio.

San Francisco

Crissy Field Marsh and Beach

The Presidio—Marina Boulevard
(415) 561–7690 / www.crissyfield.org

Hours: Café & Bookstore—9:00 a.m. to 5:00 p.m. Wednesday through Sunday

Crissy Field makes for a wonderful outing if the weather is mild. The views of the Bay and Golden Gate Bridge are phenomenal. There are pathways, meadows, marshes, and meadows that children will love to explore and parents will love to walk with or without strollers. Structured nature activities for all ages are available in the Crissy Field Center, and books and snacks can be found a the Warming Hut Cafe at the far end near the Bridge. You can join an easy one-mile walk narrated by a ranger or enroll your older children (4 and up) in a class (pre-registration is required for most). Keep an eye on your children while out and about. There are a large number of unleashed dogs around.

Crissy Field Swim Spot. On those rare sweltering San Francisco days, parents-in-the-know head to Crissy Field in the Presidio, a stunning are that includes the best swim spot in town for young kids. There is a natural lagoon on the beach that is warm enough to swim (or at least wade) in and shallow enough for toddlers and preschoolers to be able to stand in. It's great not having to worry about the riptides that make so many Bay Area beaches dangerous! The swim area is located at the end of the beach near parking, bathrooms (that have outdoor showers!), a café, and an environmental center. The only problem is that it is nearly impossible to wheel most strollers on sand, so be prepared to have to walk or carry your kids a bit to the swim area.

Food Many people start off at the Warming Hut Bookstore & Cafe, where you can also find picnics galore. The Crissy Field Center houses a small bookstore and café. You can grab breakfast or lunch and enjoy your food while looking out over the marsh in an enclosed patio, or take your food to any one of the many picnic areas.

Access MUNI 28 19th Avenue, 29 Sunset, 30 Stockton, 76 Marin Headlands

National Maritime Museum

Fisherman's Wharf—900 Beach Street
(415) 561–7100 / www.nps.gov/safr

Hours: 10:00 a.m. to 5:00 p.m. Daily

Part of the San Francisco Maritime National Historical Park, the National Maritime Museum is housed in a grand building that looks like a cruise ship. It illustrates the area's maritime past through models, photographs, paintings, and other maritime paraphernalia. Most of the exhibits, models, and photographs are not geared for the very young child, but kids may still enjoy wandering around. A new exhibit makes it possible for visitors to see, hear, and chart the movements of boats at work on the Bay. A nearby grassy area is great for a picnic. Pick up lunch at any one of the eateries in the neighborhood.

Walk from the National Maritime Museum to Hyde Street Pier via the wonderful Aquatic Park beach and promenade (see review). Or, extend your walk to Fort Point (see review). This activity is within walking distance of the shops, eateries, and amusements of Fisherman's Wharf, The Cannery, and Ghiradelli Square. You can also watch fishing off the Municipal Pier. Crafts people often set up on nearby Beach Street.

Access MUNI 19 Polk, 47 Van Ness, 49 Van Ness-Mission, F Market & Wharves historic streetcar, Powell-Hyde Cable Car

Stow Lake Boating

Golden Gate Park—Martin Luther King Drive / John F. Kennedy Drive
(415) 752–0347

Hours: 10:00 a.m. to 4:00 p.m. Monday through Friday
9:00 a.m. to 5:00 p.m. Saturday and Sunday

Fees: $14.50 for electric boat for one hour (up to 5 passengers)
$17.00 for pedal boat for one hour (up to 4 passengers)
$13.00 for rowboat (up to 4 passengers)
Cash only

This is a great activity for well-behaved preschoolers (2+) when there's one adult for each child (for safety reasons). It's a good idea to have your cell phone on you in case you get stuck or your boat steering breaks so you can call the boathouse to send rescue. The water is only three feet deep and life jackets are available. Children will enjoy steering the wheel, pointing out and feeding ducks, and going under the bridge. It takes about 30 minutes to circle the lake. Note that you may need to wait for an electric boat on weekends, and you will not be able to stow your stroller on the boat.

Activities You can also rent a covered bicycle tram (for two adults, two children – $15) on the other side of the boathouse. However, little children may not like this and it is difficult to pedal unless you have a very strong partner.

Food Snack bar (open during working hours) offers hot dogs, popcorn, soft drinks, and usual amenities.

Access MUNI 5 Fulton, 71 Haight-Noriega, 28 19th Avenue, 29 Sunset

San Francisco

Out & About: Hikes, Bikes, & Stroller Trails

San Francisco

Strybing Arboretum and Botanical Gardens
Golden Gate Park—Lincoln Way / 9th Avenue
(415) 661–1316 / www.strybing.org

Hours: 8:00 a.m. to 4:30 p.m. Monday through Friday
10:00 a.m. to 5:00 p.m. Saturday, Sunday, and National Holidays

Fees: Free. Donation suggested.

The large grassy areas (not shared by dogs) and paved walkways offer the perfect setting for crawlers, early walkers, and preschoolers to explore nature. This is a wonderful "living museum" with over 7,500 kinds of plants growing outdoors. There is a lagoon (bring bread to feed the ducks) and several water fountains that require closer supervision. It is never crowded. You can join a docent-led tour held at 1:30 p.m. daily and additional tours at 10:20 a.m. on weekends. Preschoolers will enjoy story time held at 10:30 a.m. on the first and third Sundays of each month and followed by special walks in the Arboretum at 11:00 a.m.

Food There are several kiosks selling snacks and drinks and there are restaurants in the Academy of Sciences, the Music Concourse, and on 9th Avenue and Irving Street (one block away).

Access Blue Playground, California Academy of Sciences, Japanese Tea Garden
MUNI 44 O'Shaughnessy, 71 Haight-Noriega, N Judah

More Outside Activities

Japanese Tea Garden
Golden Gate Park
(415) 752-4227

Hours: 8:30 a.m. to 6:00 p.m. Daily

Fees: Adults (12 and over) $3.50; Children (6–12) and Seniors $1.25; Under 5 Free

These quiet, well-sculpted gardens and teahouse are suitable for well-behaved preschoolers and older. Even the smallest children marvel at the intricate designs of the architecture and the beautiful grounds, especially in April when the azaleas and cherry trees bloom. You will need two adults for two children, but this can be a lot of fun for kids. They can look at the koi, climb over the tall bridge, explore the gardens, and have cookies and crackers at the teahouse. Be sure to bring milk or juice if your children don't like tea.

Activities Blue Playground, California Academy of Sciences, and Strybing Arboretum and Botanical Gardens are nearby.

Access MUNI 5 Fulton, 44 O'Shaughnessy, 71 Haight Noriega.

Yerba Buena Gardens
South of Market—Mission Street between 3rd/4th Streets
www.yerbabuena.org / Zeum/Carousel: (415) 777-2800; Skating and Bowling:
(415) 777-3727 / www.skatebowl.com

Hours: Sunrise to 10:00 p.m.; Play Circle is open during daylight hours.

Fees: Carousel is $2 for a two-ride ticket with a free ride for accompanying adults who stand beside a child (or children) under 5. 11 - 8 p.m. Carousel hours; $6.50 adul $5 12 and under

Next to Metreon (described elsewhere) and located on top of the Moscone Convention Center, Yerba Buena Gardens Rooftop is a terrific addition to San Francisco and a great place to take the whole family. There is a large grassy area with a small stage for performances (many given free, especially in summer) and the Martin Luther King Fountain, a majestic water sculpture spanning two levels that will "wow" your kids. Another fountain is located on the 3rd street side across from the Museum of Modern Art.

San Francisco

Cross over the Howard Street pedestrian bridge and find the fabulous 93 year-old hand-carved Carousel from San Francisco's Playland at the Beach. It was restored and, in addition to horses, your children can ride on giraffes, camels, and rams (11:00 a.m. to 8:00 p.m. daily; $2 for a two-ride ticket with a free ride for accompanying adults with children under five).

Walk a bit further and gaze at the intriguing interactive metal sculpture of a man sitting on a globe called Urge by Chico Macmurtrie, 1999. (Sit on the pressure sensitive bench across from the sculpture and see what happens!)

Next, on the left, you'll find one of the most unusual playgrounds in San Francisco with a couple of the best slides. Play Circle is a large circular space with rubberized cork flooring for running, jumping, ball playing, etc. (On a recent Sunday morning, there were hula-hoops and gymnastic balls provided.) The area is not fenced, but the sloping walls (also covered with rubberized cork) create a nicely contained space that includes one wide metal slide and the Play Tower that has two awesome slide tubes. (Caution: these slides are fast - a bit scary for me, but not my thrill-seeking two year-olds, despite a sign recommending use by kids 7 and older). There is also a multi-level sand/water play area with button-operated fountains, pails and shovels, and plenty of sand.

Right next door you'll find the Ice Skating Rink & Bowling Center (750 Folsom Street), offering ice skating classes for those as young as age three and a small bowling alley that welcomes families. Classes are held in six- or eight-week series and cost anywhere from $75.00 to $140.00. The bowling alley (Adults $4.00 game, Children 12 and under $2.50/game, Shoe Rental $2.50 for all ages, 10:00 a.m. to 10:00 p.m. Sunday through Thursday and 10:00 a.m. to midnight Friday and Saturday. Limited Tuesday and Thursday after 6:00 p.m.) allows you to simply push a button to eliminate gutter balls and make it easy for children as young as two who can push the ball to have a great time.

Zeum, a hands-on participatory environment for youth arts expression, is best for kids eight and older.

Food

PICNIC: Metreon has many restaurants, including the extremely child friendly Into the Night Kitchen (on the upper floor with views of SFMOMA and the growing South of Market skyline); on top of the bowling alley you can find Mo's Grill, a gourmet burger joint; a less expensive alternative is to pick up sandwiches in the Starbucks on the upper level of the Gardens or bring your own and picnic on the grass.

MAKE A DAY:

Access

MUNI Underground to Powell Street or MUNI 14 Mission bus; parking at 5th and Mission Garage; very stroller friendly with ramps or elevators.

Amusements

Basic Brown Bear Factory

Potrero Hill—444 DeHaro Street/Mariposa Street
(800) 554.1910/www.basicbrownbear.com

Hours: 10:00 a.m. to 5:00 p.m. Monday through Saturday
12:00 p.m. to 5:00 p.m. Sundays

Fees: Free drop-in tour 1:00 p.m. daily
Additional free drop-in tour 11:00 a.m. Saturdays

This is the place that kids (preschoolers and older best) can learn about and create their own teddy bears! The 30-minute tour consists of a brief teddy bear history, demonstrations of how a pattern is made and cut, how the bears are sewn, then how they are stuffed and fluffed. Kids pick their own teddy bear in a variety of colors and textures (prices start at $12 - there's no obligation to buy if you're not interested). With assistance from a "factory worker", hook up teddy to an antique stuffing machine (a tube runs into teddy's armpit) and the kids use a foot pump to stuff him (takes about 10 seconds). They then run teddy through a blowing machine to give him a "bear bath" (remove the fuzz). Even at 2-1/2 years old, kids can work the pump (you can assist them with the pumping if they're too small), though they may find the machine too noisy and scary. Then choose an outfit if you'd like or just add a ribbon (there are over 40 outfits available), help the kids dress their bear, and you're ready to go!

Food

Several cafes are located a couple of blocks down on DeHaro Street. Just one block away is the newly-renovated Jackson Playground (see earlier description).

Access

MUNI 19 Polk, 22

Metreon – a Sony Entertainment Center

Yerba Buena /South of Market—101 4th Street
(800) metreon or (415) 369.6000 / www.metreon.com

Hours: Metreon—10:00 a.m. to 10:00 p.m. Where the Wild Things Are—10:00 a.m.
to 7:00 p.m. Friday and Saturday, 10:00 a.m. to 6:00 p.m. Sunday and Monday
In the Night Kitchen—11:00 a.m. to 7:00 p.m. Friday and Saturday. 11:00 a.m.
to 5:00 p.m. Sunday and Monday
Times for Where the Wild Things Are and In the Night Kitchen change according to
school schedules, so be sure to call ahead.

San Francisco

Fees: **Metreon**—Free
Where the Wild Things Are—Four and older $6

Although Metreon is a great place to go with children of all ages, especially when it's raining, it is geared more towards pre-teens, teenagers, and adults. However, it is possible to visit Metreon and have a great time with your toddler exploring all four floors and paying a visit to Where the Wild Things Are. If your child can sit through movies, take in a movie on the biggest IMAX theater screen in North America.

Where the Wild Things Are is a play space made from characters and props from the popular Maurice Sendak book. The whole child is involved as they walk through this hands-on, interactive attraction. Many younger children find the first part of this attraction scary—dark with lots of noises. However, you can skip the first part and enter the exhibit backward. The last part of the attraction is a fun play space with huge blocks, a boat, and a slide. It has lots of space for running and jumping and makes a terrific rainy day activity.

Be sure to visit during the holidays (Thanksgiving to January 1). Beginning at noon and happening on the hour every hour until 6:00 p.m., snow will fall inside the Metreon. Kids love playing in the snow, and parents love not having to put on parkas and mittens and boots!

Food   The Metreon has many restaurants, including the extremely child friendly In the Night Kitchen (on the upper floor outside Where the Wild Things Are with views of SFMOMA and the growing South of Market skyline). A less expensive alternative is to pick up sandwiches in Starbucks and eat on the upper level of the gardens.

Access   MUNI Underground to Powell Street, 14 Mission

Musee Mechanique
Pier 45
(415) 386.1170 / www.coin-opcollector.com/Musee.htm

Hours: 11:00 a.m. to 7:00 p.m. Monday through Friday
10:00 a.m. to 8:00 p.m. Saturday and Holidays

Fees: Free (10¢ to 50¢ to play mechanical machines and games)

Locals often overlooked this tiny museum, which has been housed at the Cliff House. However, when it was recently evicted, locals created such an outcry −52,000 emails worth− that Musee Mechanique was saved and relocated to Pier 45. It is truly a treasure of San Francisco. This near-century-old institution houses over a hundred mechanical games and playthings mainly created between the 1890s through the 1930s. There are several player pianos (children are fascinated by this), many games for twins to compete against each other (fireman's ladder, golf games, soccer kicking, bicycle racing, all from the 1920's genre and earlier), two Fortune teller gypsies (think "Big"), many MutoScopes (one with black and white footage from the 1906 earthquake), mechanical life displays such as a "Day on the Farm" and "At the Carnival" (both about 6' x 10' in glass enclosed booth with dozens of activities going on at once), "Love" tester (squeeze the grip and see how "hot" you are), an arm wrestling machine, Santa's Workshop, "Laughing Sal" from the old Playland at the Beach (8 foot woman in a glass booth who both delights and frightens with her crazy psycho laugh), and so much more. Most games are 25¢, although a few are 50¢ (change machines available at the museum). Adults may be more interested than the children, but it will definitely hold a kid's interest.

Because the new Musee Mechanique was slated to open October 2002, we are unable to offer hints on parking, double-stroller accessibility, and the like.

Pier 39

Fisherman's Wharf—The Embarcadero and Beach Street
(415) 981.7437 / www.PIER39.com

Hours:	Summer—10:00 am to 9:00 p.m. Monday through Friday
	10:00 a.m. to 10:00 p.m. Saturday and Sunday
	Fall and Spring—11:00 am to 8:00 p.m. Monday through Friday
	10:00 am to 8:30 p.m. Saturday and Sunday
	Winter—11:00 a.m. to 7:00 p.m. Monday through Friday
	11:00 a.m. to 8:00 p.m. Saturday and Sunday

Pier 39 has plenty to look at, buy, eat, and experience. Highlights for adults include restaurants and shops and fabulous views of Alcatraz, the Golden Gate and Bay Bridges, and the city's skyline. Highlights for kids include watching the sea lions sun themselves on K-dock, petting the sharks in Aquarium of the Bay (see review), watching street performers, and riding on the two-tiered Venetian Carousel (be forewarned that sometimes the operators require one adult ride per small child). The Marine Mammal Center provides free educational talks regarding the sea lions on weekends 11:00 a.m. to 5:00 p.m.

There are numerous restaurants along Pier 39.   **Food**

Ferries to Alcatraz, Angel Island, Sausalito, and Tiburon leave from   **Activities**
nearby piers. A small, unfenced playground-type climbing structure is
found to the right of Pier 39.

MUNI F Market & Wharves historic streetcar   **Access**

Trains, Planes, & Automobiles

San Francisco

Golden Gate Railroad Museum
Hunters Point—Hunters Point Shipyard, Building 809
(415) 822.8728 or 650.363.2472 / www.ggrm.org

Hours: 10:00 a.m. to 4:00 p.m. Saturday and Sunday

Fees: Adults $5.00, Youth (8 and older) $2.00, Children (7 and under) free

This museum is really best for preschoolers and older, although toddlers might find it entertaining if your family is fanatical about trains. The museum is dedicated to the preservation of vintage steam and diesel locomotives and passenger equipment. It owns and operates many locomotives related to Bay Area railroads. You can walk through a number of display cars and locomotives. It is a working museum, so a lot of equipment is in the process of being worked on. The Golden Gate Railroad Museum has a nice small gift store with fun and well-priced train paraphernalia.

Food   A snack bar with beverages and limited snacks is in one of the cars.

Access   Hwy 101 to Cesar Chavez Street (Army Street), to Evans Avenue to Hunters Point Shipyard, Building 809. Need vehicle registration, proof of insurance and picture ID for admission to shipyard.

Hyde Street Pier
Fisherman's Wharf
(415) 561.7100 / www.nps.gov/safr

Hours: 9:30 a.m. to 5:00 p.m. Daily

Fees: Walkway—Free
Ships—Adult $5.00, 17 and under free

Hyde Street Pier offers tours of six historic vessels, including a ferryboat, schooners, and tugboats. Many of the boats are accessibly by stroller. Much of the history associated with the boats will be lost on children under the age of 6, but kids of all ages will enjoy just walking the pier and looking at the boats. The Maritime Store of Hyde Street Pier offers books, games, models, videos, and posters. Proceeds help support educational programs and conservation projects.
Be mindful of the child-size gaps in the fence on Hyde Street Pier.

There is also a small area leading to the water to the right of the rowing club that is not fenced.

Walk from Hyde Street Pier to the National Museum via the wonderful Aquatic Park beach and promenade (see review). This activity is within walking distance of the shops, eateries, and amusements of Fisherman's Wharf, The Cannery, and Ghiradelli Square. You can also watch fishing off the Municipal Pier. Crafts people often set up on nearby Beach Street.

A nearby grassy area is great for a picnic. Pick up lunch at any one of the eateries in the neighborhood.

MUNI 19 Polk, 47 Van Ness, 49 Van Ness-Mission,

F Market & Wharves historic streetcar, Powell-Hyde Cable Car

Access

San Francisco

Little Puffer

The Sunset—San Francisco Zoo, Sloat Boulevard/45th Avenue
(415) 753.7080 / www.sfzoo.org

Hours: Summer—10:00 a.m. to 5:00 p.m. Daily
Spring, Fall, & Winter—10:00 a.m. to 5:00 p.m. Saturday and Sunday

Fees: $2.00 for all over 3

The Little Puffer steam train, operated by San Francisco Zoo (see review), circles the zoo and is great for all ages. It goes twice around the track, through a tunnel, and onto the trestle bridge.

San Francisco Cable Car Museum

Nob Hill—1201 Mason Street
(415) 474.1887 (museum) and (415) 923.6162 (railway) /
www.cablecarmuseum.com

Hours: April through September—10:00 a.m. to 6:00 p.m. daily
October through March—10:00 a.m. through 5:00 p.m. daily
Closed Thanksgiving Day, Christmas Day, and New Year's Day

Fee: Donations appreciated

Located in the historic San Francisco cable car barn and powerhouse, the museum allows visitors to view the actual cable winding machinery. Included in the displays are three antique cable cars and the first cable car (built in 1873). This is really best for preschoolers and older children.

F Market

Access

East Bay

The prime purpose of being four is to enjoy being four

- of secondary importance is to prepare for being five.

Jim Trelease,
The Read-Aloud Handbook

There are no seven wonders of the world in the eyes of a child.

There are seven million.

Walt Streightiff

Parks & Playgrounds

East Bay

Adventure Playground
Berkeley—160 University Avenue
(510) 644–8623 / www.ci.berkeley.ca.us

Hours: School Year—11:00 a.m. to 4:00 p.m. Saturday, Sunday, and Holidays
Summer—9:00 a.m. to 5:00 p.m. Monday through Friday
11:00 a.m. to 5:00 p.m. Saturday and Sunday

Fees: Children accompanied by adults are free
Children age 7 and up without adult $5.00 for up to three hours

If your kids are rugged and you are bored with the usual metal and plastic playgrounds, put on old clothes and sturdy, closed-toe shoes and give aptly-named Adventure Playground a try. This one-of-a-kind place—open since 1978—allows older kids to add to the play environment by hammering, sawing, and painting. Tools and construction are continuously checked by safety-conscious city-paid employees.

Although the playground is geared for older kids, closely supervised younger children who are expert climbers and who are within arms length of their parents can have a great time wandering around the aging wooden structures and climbing on the cargo net. Other attractions include a zipline (ages 6 and older), a rope swing, and a tire wall.

Children 7 years and older may stay in the playground without their parents for up to three hours. Registration is required and parents must sign their children in and out.

Food Sandwiches, snacks, and smoothies can be obtained at nearby Seabreeze Market or restaurants Skates on the Bayor His Lordships. The Adventure Playground is also close to Berkeley's fabulous 4th Street shopping district.

Make a Day After a visit to the Adventure Playgroud, take some time to watch the windsurfers, wander on the pier, or go to Shorebird Nature Center.

Driving I-80 E/I-580 W to University Avenue exit towards Berkeley. Right onto University Avenue

Aquatic Park Playground
Berkeley—Bolivar Drive/Bancroft Way
(510) 649–9874 / www.bpfp.org

The playground in Aquatic Park is wonderfully unique and great for toddlers and older children. Children from Berkeley's elementary schools

were asked for their wildest ideas for a playground and architect Bob Leathers translated their dreams into plans. Those plans took shape during the summer of 2000 as over 2,000 volunteers built the "Dream Land for Kids" at Aquatic Park. The playground consists of a series of wooden structures with castle-like turrets, elevated play spaces on multiple levels, mazes, ramps, and slides. There is a separate structure for toddlers with infant swings.The playground is underlain by wood chips, is semi-enclosed on a secluded dead-end street, and includes a working garden. The Southern Pacific and Amtrak railway passes directly behind the playground and although the whistles are a delight to train-lovers, they can be unnerving for children sensitive to loud noises.

Food Fun food and shopping can be found on Berkeley's 4th Street

Driving I-80 E/I-580 W to University Avenue exit towards Berkeley. Hard right onto 2nd Street. Right onto Addison Street. Left onto Bolivar Drive.

Central Park

San Ramon—12501 Alcosta Blvd.
(925) 973–3200 / www.ci.san-ramon.ca.us

This is the king of playgrounds and is considered well worth driving long distances to spend time here. Crawlers to older children will enjoy this beautiful park and its many facilities. The playground consists of two extensive play structures underlain by sand, separated by a fabulous fountain and a meandering shallow rock creek where even young kids can play safely. A low concrete bench surrounds the playground and keeps the kids contained within. San Ramon is usually quite warm, so come with bathing suit, buckets, and shovels. Central Park also features baseball/softball diamonds, soccer fields, and basketball and tennis courts.

Food Central park has picnic areas, and you can pick up some lunch at the nearby Whole Foods Market. The adjacent shopping mall includes Borders Books and Whole Foods Market.

Driving Hwy 680 S to Bollinger Canyon Road exit. Left onto Bollinger Canyon Road. Right onto Alcosta Boulevard.

Civic Park

Walnut Creek—1375 Civic Drive/North Broadway Street
(925) 943–5852 / www.ci.walnut-creek.ca.us

This large playground has numerous structures that are fun for early walkers to older children to explore. The playground is underlain by sand and includes a water play area and several infant and regular swings.

East Bay

and a grassy area separate the parking lot from the playground. Park covers 10 acres and features a softball field, tennis courts, unity center, a native plant/butterfly habitat garden with over 25 of butterflies and 130 species of native California plants, and Arts Education. It also includes connections to the Iron Horse and Creek Walk.

Food Park includes picnic areas, so grab lunch at nearby Broadway Plaza or downtown Walnut Creek which is just one block away.

Driving Hwy 680 S towards Mt. Diablo Boulevard. Continue on Mt. Diablo Boulevard. Left onto N. California Boulevard. Right onto Civic Drive.

Community Center Playground and Park
Orinda—26 Orinda Way
(925) 254–2445 / www.ci.orinda.ca.us

Orinda's Community Center Park includes two play structures—one recently renovated for early walkers to toddlers and underlain by sand. It includes infant and toddler swings, a tire swing, and a sand/water play area. The second climbing structure is designed specifically for children 5 years and younger and is made of wood and underlain by sand. An additional play structure is to be added by spring 2003 for children 6 years and older.

The play area is enclosed only by the park fence and is adjacent to a large grassy area that is shared with dogs but is usually clean. The playground gets crowded mid-morning.

Make a Day The park is located in Orinda Village with shopping (grocery, drugstore, great bookstore, several eateries) within easy walking distance. A farmers' market is held on Saturdays during the summer. You can also take your children across the street to the fire station where they are very welcomed. In addition, a concert series is held Tuesday evenings in the summer.

Driving CA-24 East to Camino Pablo exit. Left onto Camino Pablo. Right onto Santa Maria Way. Left onto Orinda Way.

Heather Farm Park
Walnut Creek—301 N. San Carlos Dr
(925) 943–5858 / www.ci.walnut-creek.ca.us

This 102-acre park includes duck ponds, the Clarke Memorial Swim Center (see review), tennis courts, picnic areas, ball fields, a community center, and bike paths. There is a semi-fenced playground with older

East Bay

climbing structures over sand and infant swings. There are better playgrounds in the area, but the rest of the park is lovely. The Gardens at Heather Farm (1540 Marchbanks Dr, 925.947.1678) are free and offer a beautifully landscaped 5.4-acre educational garden. The park does get busy on weekends.

Driving I-680 N towards Ygnacio Valley Road. Right onto Ygnacio Valley Road. Left onto N. San Carlos Drive.

Larkey Park

Walnut Creek—Buena Vista Avenue/First Avenue
(925) 943–5858 / www.ci.walnut-creek.ca.us

You can make a day of it in this 13-acre park. It includes two playground areas. The first area is geared towards toddlers and includes small, simple structures such as a slide, merry-go-round, and infant swings underlain by sand. The second structure, for preschoolers and older, is a tall metal climbing structure with tunnel slides and jungle gym features. It is also underlain by sand. Both playgrounds are surrounded by a wide grassy strip. And, though there are no fences, children are safely separated from the road.

Make a Day The park also includes bike paths, tennis courts, a swim center (see review), and the excellent Lindsay Wildlife Museum (see review).

Food Larkey Park has picnic areas and food can be bought nearby in Walnut Creek–about a mile from the park.

Driving I-680 N. to Geary Boulevard exit. Geary Boulevard to Buena Vista Avenue.

Montclair Village Park

Montclair Village—Moraga and Thornhill
(510) 649–9874 / www.montclairvillage.com

This park has a variety of play structures including a fenced area for 0-5 year olds. There is also a duck pond in the middle of the pond which can be fun but is not fenced; therefore, parents need to be very aware of their children when near the pond.

Food Montclair Village is nearby, so food choices are plentiful. There is a Noah's bagels along with every major coffee house. The Montclair Egg Shop is in the village, and if your children are interested in trains, this is the place for them! It is open for breakfast and lunch and is VERY kid friendly!

Driving South—Hwy 13 to Thornhill/Moraga exit. North—Hwy 13 to Park Boulevard exit. Head left.

East Bay

East Bay

Moraga Commons Park

Moraga—St. Mary's Road/Moraga Road
(925) 376–2520

This sunny and immaculately clean park—"whenever we visit, someone is either cleaning the picnic grounds, planting flowers, or doing some other form of maintenance"—contains two playgrounds and a water play/sprinkler area. The one closest to the parking lot is for infants/toddlers and has a new metal/rubber structure with coarse sand, two infant swings, and an adjacent play-train structure for extra fun. The second structure (further away from the parking lot and with a wood chip base) is for 4+ years, but younger kids can play on it safely too. It includes more challenging jungle gym equipment. The two areas are separated by a large grassy field perfect for running or picnicking. Plus, a terrific water area includes two fountains that spray water into the air so kids can run through it (like running through sprinklers only better). The water area has a cement base and operates in the summer months only. Although the Commons is surrounded by a large grassy area, the enclosing low wood-rail fence can be penetrated by a wandering toddler, so keep your children in view at all times.

There is a sand volleyball court and bocce ball court, plus a lovely amphitheater where families can enjoy a FREE live concert every Thursday evening for 12 weeks in the summer months. Moraga Commons is one of the trailheads for the Moraga-Lafayette Trail (see review).

Driving Hwy 24 east to Orinda exit. Right onto Moraga Way. Left onto Moraga Road. Right onto St. Mary's Road.

Oak Hill Park

Danville—3005 Stone Valley Road
(925) 314–3400

This is a pretty park with a small but nice playground for toddlers. It is next to a duck pond and large grassy areas. The simple equipment is made of wood and metal and is underlain by sand. The playground includes infant swings, some little rocking horses, and easy climbing structures. The play area is not fenced, but is confined by a semi-circular hill that rises behind it. A path runs through the park and is a good place to practice bike riding.

Driving I-680 south to Solano Way exit. Right onto Solano Way. Continue on Stone Valley Road.

Osage Station Park

Danville—816 Brookside Drive
(925) 314-3400 / www.ci.danville.ca.us

The playground in this lovely park with shade trees is great for early walkers through preschoolers. The play equipment includes a little train and wooden structures with a train station and western-town motif. One of the play structures is geared for preschoolers with lots of levels to explore. The playground has a wonderful waterfall and running rock-lined shallow *creek* for kids to play in—a great place to cool down. The water runs into a large shallow pool about one foot deep, so little tikes will need some extra supervision. The play area is semi-enclosed by a low concrete bench and underlain by sand. The playground does not include swings.

Osage Station Park is known for its beautiful memorial rose garden. The park features four tennis courts, four baseball diamonds, several soccer fields, plus a path around the park. The park can be crowded on weekend mornings.

You can pick up lunch at the small shopping center on Diablo Road near the highway and head to the picnic area in the park.

I-680 S to Sycamore Valley Road exit. Turn right on Brookside Drive.   **Driving**

Pleasant Hill Park

Pleasant Hill—Gregory Lane/Cleaveland Road
(925) 682-0896 / www.pleasanthillrec.com

The playground in Pleasant Hill Park includes newer play structures with metal and plastic frames, underlain by sand and wood chips, that are great for toddlers and older children. However, some of the older play structures are appropriate for younger children. Infant and regular swings are located a few hundred feet from the playground. The playground isn't fenced, but it is separated from the road by a large grassy area and the entire playground is easily viewable. Pleasant Hill Park features softball fields, volleyball/basketball courts, and a swimming center.

Pleasant Hill Park includes picnic areas, so grab lunch along Contra Costa Boulevard or in the new Pleasant Hill Shopping Center.

A number of mega-stores, including Borders, Bed, Bath and Beyond, and Michaels Art Store is located in the Pleasant Hill Shopping Center.

I-680 N to Contra Costa Boulevard exit towards Pleasant Hill. Right onto N. Main   **Driving**
Street. Continue on Contra Costa Boulevard. Left onto Gregory Lane.

East Bay

Totland

Berkeley—Virginia Street/McGee Avenue
(510) 981-6700 / www.ci.berkeley.ca.us

Totland is an excellent destination for toddlers—completely fenced with latching gates—but is also okay for early walkers. It is located in a quiet Berkeley neighborhood and is surrounded by a grassy area. The new metal and plastic toddler playground structure has elevated play spaces and slides, all underlain by clean sand. It also includes infant swings, a sand play area, and a water play area. The playground has lots of used toys, donated by the community, for use by all young visitors. The playground is crowded from 10:30 a.m. to noon.

Picnic tables are located under shade trees, and food can be found at the Hopkins Avenue shopping district or on the Shattuck Avenue commercial strip (restaurants, bakery, banks and more.)

I-80 E/I-580 W to University Avenue exit towards Berkeley. Right onto University Avenue. Left onto Sacramento Street. Right onto Virginia Street.

Totlot Playground

Lafayette—500 St. Mary's Road
(925) 284-2232 / www.lafayette.govoffice.com

This is a small but functional playground, fully enclosed and gated, with small, older wooden climbing structures and tree house on sand. There are no swings. It is best for early walkers and toddlers. Totlot is also used by the Lafayette Tot-Drop Center, where residents can drop off their children for a few hours of childcare.

Access to the Moraga-Lafayette Trail is nearby.

Driving CA-24 E to Oak Hill Road exit. Right onto Oak Hill Road. Left onto Mt Diablo Boulevard. Right onto Moraga Road. Left onto St. Mary's Road.

East Bay

Animals: Zoos, Farms & Nature Centers

Ardenwood Historic Farm
Fremont—34600 Ardenwood Blvd.
(510) 796–0663 / www.ebparks.org

Hours: Labor Day through Memorial Day—10:00 a.m. to 4:00.p.m. Tuesday through
Sunday

Fee: Tuesday, Wednesday, Saturday—Adult (18+) $1.00, Youth (4–17)
50¢, under 4 free
Thursday, Friday, Sunday—Adult (18+) $5.00, Youth (13-17) $4.00, Child (4–12)
$3.50, under 4 free

A visit to Ardenwood is a journey back to the time of the Patterson
Ranch —a prosperous, 205-acre 19th century country farming estate
including a beautiful mansion and its elaborate Victorian Gardens. Today
the Historic Farm exhibits agricultural practices from the 1870s to the
present, demonstrating the transition from horse-powered to horsepower.
Kids of all ages will especially enjoy the many animals in the Farm Yard,
as well as wagon rides and a unique horse-drawn railroad (see review).
There are special events, throughout the year such as an old-fashioned
Independence Day celebration, summer and fall harvest festivals, special
music concerts, recreation of Victorian social events, and Ardenwood's
Victorian Christmas in December.
You can grab lunch at the Farmyard Cafe.   **Food**
CA–84 W to Ardenwood/Newark Boulevard exit. Right onto Ardenwood   **Driving**
Boulevard.

East Bay

Dunsmuir House and Garden
Oakland—2960 Peralta Oaks Court
(510) 615–5555 / www.dunsmuir.org

Hours: February through December—10:00 a.m. to 4:00 p.m. Tuesday through Friday

Fee: Free

This 50-acre historic estate includes the Dunsmuir House mansion,
landscaped grounds, and a farm area with an historic carriage house. The
grounds are lovely to stroll—perfect for young walkers. During the

Christmas Holidays, the house is transformed and visitors can listen to carolers, go for carriage rides, and visit Father Christmas. Children can even have tea with Father Christmas (advanced registration required). Special hours and prices do apply during most of December, so call ahead and check.

Food An indoor pavilion offers limited refreshments on weekends.

Driving I-580 East to 106th Ave./Foothill Blvd. exit. Make three left turns at the three stop signs. Drive under freeway and turn right onto Peralta Oaks Dr. Follow signs to Dunsmuir. Or, I-580 W to Foothill/MacArthur Blvd. Move into the right lane as you drive under the freeway and continue right onto Foothill Blvd. Make a right turn at the next stop sign onto 106th Ave. Drive under freeway and turn right onto Peralta Oaks Dr. Follow signs to Dunsmuir.

Lindsay Wildlife Museum

Walnut Creek—1931 First Avenue
(925) 935–1978 / www.wildlife-museum.org

Hours: June 17 through September 3—10:00 a.m. to 5:00 p.m. Tuesday through Sunday
Remainder of Year—12:00 p.m. to 5:00 p.m. Tuesday through Friday;
10:00 a.m. to 5:00 p.m. Saturday and Sunday
Closed Holidays

Fee: Adults (18+) $5.00, Children (3 –17) $4.00, under 3 free

Although Lindsay Wildlife Museum is OK for younger children, it is most appropriate for toddlers and older. This high quality museum specializes in wildlife rehabilitation and habitat restoration in urban areas. A 35-ft replica of "Balancing Rock" from the top of Mt Diablo displays native California animals and plants. Bald eagle and bobcat feedings are held daily. The "Especially for Children" area provides a space for young children to learn about animals found in their own community. The facility includes a wildlife hospital—one of the oldest and largest in the United States—and Pet Library (animals can be checked out for short periods of time). Children can also pet pocket pets, such as rabbits, hamsters, rats, and guinea pigs. The museum offers a wide array of classes for children and their caregivers from the age of 2.

Food The nearest place to buy food is at the Palo Verde Shopping Center (Lunardi's Market) at the intersection of Geary and Pleasant Hill Rd, or at the other end of Geary Rd near Hwy 680, where there are several fast food concessions. Have your lunch in Larkey Park.

Make a Day Lindsay Wildlife Museum is next to the Larkey Park playgrounds (toddler and preschooler structures—see review).

Driving Hwy 24 to North Pleasant Hill Road exit. Continue on Pleasant Hill. Continue straight on Geary. Turn right onto Buena Vista. Right onto First Avenue.

Litte Farm & Environmental Education Center

Berkeley—Tilden Park near Jewel Lake
(510) 525–2233 / www.ebparks.org

Hours: Farm—8:30 a.m. to 4:00 p.m. Daily
Education Center—10:00 a.m. to 5:00 p.m. Tuesday through Sunday

Little Farm contains friendly livestock and farm implements. The animal residents, which include pigs, goats, cows, and sheep enjoy eating from young visitors' hands, so be sure to pack some celery or lettuce for your visit. Adjacent to the Little Farm is the small but interesting Environmental Educational Center, with exhibits of local wildlife and history. Visitors can also take a short walk around Jewel Lake, or ride on the ponies (510) 527–0421; $2.50 per ride or $23 for 10 rides; 11:00 a.m. to 5:00 p.m. weekends during school year and 11:00 a.m. to 4:00 p.m. during school summer vacation) just a short walk through the parking lot. A small playground structure is adjacent to the parking lot.
The Tilden merry-go-round is near the southern turn-off to the Nature Center from Wildcat Canyon Road. The merry-go-round is an antique carousel with hand-carved and beautifully painted wooden carousel animals (510) 524–6773; $1.00 per ride or $10 for 13-ride ticket book; 11:00 a.m. to 5:00 p.m. Saturday and Sunday only after Labor Day and daily during school spring and summer vacation). The tranquil Lake Anza (see description elsewhere) is also nearby. The Little Train (see description elsewhere), another favorite destination, is on the southern end of Tilden Park, off Grizzley Peak Rd (follow signs within the park). There is a small food concession stand at the merry-go-round, but no others in Tilden Regional Park.

Hwy 80 to Albany exit. Right onto Marin Avenue.. Continue on Marin. Left onto **Driving** Grizzley Park. Right onto Wildcat Canyon Road. Follow signs.

East Bay

Oakland Zoo

Oakland—9777 Golf Links Road at 98th Avenue
(510) 632–9525 / www.oaklandzoo.org

Hours: 10:00 a.m. to 4:00 p.m. Daily.
Closed Thanksgiving Day and Christmas Day

Fees: Parking $3.00
Adult (15–55) $7.50, Child (2–14) $4.50, under 2 free,
Free with San Francisco Zoo membership.

The 100-acre Oakland Zoo is a great alternative to the San Francisco Zoo as is often has better weather and is less spread out—although slightly hilly—making it easy for even a toddler to walk through most of the exhibits. The Zoo has been undergoing a renovation over the past few years and many of the animals are now exhibited in large and interesting range areas. The Gibbon Island display is a hoot (literally!). The Zoo has an African-themed area with a tunnel into a meerkat colony, perfect for exploring toddlers. Besides the African and Austral-Asia animals of the zoo, there's a small petting zoo (in need of repairs). Rides include the Sky Ride (need two parents for this, $2.00 for each) that offers a great view of the animal park and the East Bay, as well as an Oakland Zoo Train. A small amusement ride area near the zoo includes a new endangered species carousel, roller coaster, plane and car rides, and a great miniature train that also offers splendid views. The ride area is open 11:00 a.m. to 4:00 p.m. daily and rides cost 75¢ to $2.00 each. Plans for the future include remodeling the children's zoo.

Food A small café near the zoo entrance offers limited but adequate fare; picnickers are limited to large grassy area near petting zoo or park benches in amusement ride area.

Driving I-580 E to 98th Avenue/Gold Links Road exit. Left onto Golf Links Road.

East Bay

Old Borges Ranch

Walnut Creek—Shell Ridge Open Space, 1035 Castle Rock Road
(925) 934–6990 / www.walnut-creek.org

Hours: Ranch—Daily
Visitor center—1:00 p.m. to 4:00 p.m. Saturday
12:00 p.m. to 4:00 p.m. 1st Sunday of the month

Fee: Donations appreciated

This working cattle ranch (sheep, horses, goats, geese, pigs, cattle, and chickens) is best for toddlers and older. The Borges Ranch is a national historic site where historic buildings can be viewed along with the ranch animals.

Near the trailhead of Castle Rock trail (requires a jog-stroller).

I-680 N to Ignacio Valley exit. East on Ignacio Valley. Right onto Walnut Avenue. Right onto Castle Rock Road. Or, I-680 S to Oak Pack turnoff. Left onto Main. Quick left onto Treat Boulevard. Right onto Bancroft. Continue on Walnut Avenue.

Sulphur Creek Nature Center

Hayward—1801 D St.
(510) 881–6747 / www.hard.dst.ca.us

Hours: 10:00 a.m. to 5:00 p.m. Tuesday through Sunday

Fee: Per person $4.00

Sulphur Creek Nature Center is a wildlife education and rehabilitation facility where children can learn about native Californian species. The museum includes exhibits of smaller creatures such as salamanders, amphibians and reptiles, while outside displays include coyote, opossums, foxes and birds of prey in a wildlife garden. On Saturday and Sundays at 2:30 p.m., the docents bring out animals for interactive discussions. The exhibits change regularly. The nature center offers classes for toddlers and up, and has an animal lending library program. Although the museum and garden are stroller-friendly, there is a short trail that goes out from the center that is accessible by foot only.

Pick up lunch in downtown Hayward and have a picnic at the center.   **Food**

I-580 E to Redwood Road exit. Right onto Redwood Road. Continue on A Street.   **Driving**
Left onto 4th Street. Left onto D Street.

East Bay

Museums: Art, Science & Hands-on

Chabot Space and Science Center
Oakland—10000 Skyline Blvd.
(510) 336-7300 / www.chabotspace.org

Hours: Summer Hours—10:00 a.m. to 5:00 p.m. Tuesday through Thursday
10:00 a.m. to 9:00 p.m. Friday and Saturday
12:00 p.m. to 5:00 p.m. Sunday
School Hours—10:00 a.m. to 3:00 p.m. Tuesday through Thursday
10:00 a.m. to 7:30 p.m. Friday and Saturday
12:00 p.m. to 5:00 p.m. Sunday.
Closed Thanksgiving Day and Christmas Day
Planetarium & Theater evening hours: 7:30 p.m. to 9:00 p.m. Friday and Saturday

Fees: Parking fee $4.00
General Admission —Adult (13+) $8.00, Youth (4–12) $5.50
GA + One Venue (Planetarium or Theatre)—Adult $14.75, Youth $11.00
GA + Two Venues (Planetarium and Theatre)—Adult $19.75, Youth $15.50
Planetarium & Theatre tickets cannot be purchased separately from GA
except during Friday and Saturday evening hours—Adult $8.75, Youth $6.50
Beginning January 1, 2002, reciprocal memberships will be good for 50% off of
General Admission.

Chabot Space and Science Center is an astronomy lovers dream! It is set high in the Oakland hills and its exhibits focus on the earth's solar system, space exploration, and earth processes. It includes exciting, but pricey, planetarium and theater shows.

Younger children may not be able to understand most of the exhibits, but they'll enjoy roaming the two floors, playing with the sculptures named Planetary Landscapes, and visiting the hands-on play room. Planetary Landscapes have lots of buttons, cranks, and touch-sensitive surfaces that manipulate sand, air, fluid, and heat to represent natural geologic phenomena. The play room is appropriate for early walkers on up as it has building blocks, soft toys, a couple of animal exhibits (turtles and frogs) a coloring/collage section, and more. It is sometimes used for birthday parties, but the public is still welcome to use it during the parties.

If your kids happen to be obsessed with the Solar System or are six or older, they'll love it. Preschoolers through second graders will also enjoy Discovery Lab–a hands-on play space with science experiments, telescopes, and much more. However, be sure to check the hours of the Discovery Lab before visiting.

Chabot has wide, long halls that make keeping track of children very easy, and it is rarely crowded. It is best for walkers and olders, as

double-strollers can be used but not with ease. There is a great gift shop that has space related games and educational toys.
A small café serves coffee and snacks and there is an outdoor sitting area overlooking a beautiful California native plants garden. **Food**
I-580 E to 35th Avenue exit. Left onto 35th Avenue. Continue on Redwood Road. Left onto Skyline. **Getting There**

Habitot Children's Museum
Berkeley—2065 Kittredge St.
(510) 647–1111 / www.habitot.org

Hours: 9:30 a.m. to 1:00 p.m. Monday and Wednesday; 9:30 a.m. to 5:00 p.m. Tuesday and Friday; 9:30 a.m. to 7:00 p.m. Thursday; 10:00 a.m. to 5:00 p.m. Saturday; 11:00 a.m. to 5:00 p.m. Sunday between Labor Day through Memorial. Closed on most major holidays

Fees: First child 7 and under $6.00, Additional children 7 and under $3.00, Adults $4.00, 9 months and under free
Family membership $70.

This relatively new hands-on museum where young children can actively explore their imagination in a 4,000 sq. ft. area that has only one guarded entrance is great for crawlers through preschoolers. Habitot offers exhibits that encourage children to discover art, water play, music, science, and dress-up play. Dress your children in clothes that can get dirty and wet and bring an extra change of clothes. A separate area for crawlers is off-limits for older kids. Habitot is one of the few activities that offers exhibits where babies can crawl around and see different colors and shapes. The museum is most crowded around 10:30 a.m. to 12:00 p.m. (particularly on rainy days) and on Fridays (the dreaded field-trip day).
Food on nearby Shattuck Ave. (downtown Berkeley) commercial strip. **Food**
I-80 E/I-580 W to Ashby Avenue/Shellmound Street/CA-13. Continue on Ashby **Driving**
Avenue. Bear left on Adeline Street. Continue on Shattuck Avenue. Left onto Kittredge Street.

East Bay

Lawrence Hall of Science

Berkeley—Centennial Drive, UC Berkeley Campus
(510) 642–5132 / www.lhs.berkeley.edu

Hours: 10:00 a.m. to 5:00 p.m. Daily
Closed Thanksgiving Day and Christmas Day

Fee: Adults (19+) $8.00, Youth (5–18) $6.00; Child (3–4) $4.00; Under 2 free
Reciprocal with other Bay Area science museums.

This is an excellent destination for all scientists at heart, especially toddlers, preschoolers, and older. This family museum includes hands-on exhibits that allow children to explore the natural world as well as the celestial reaches. Several areas are geared toward young visitors, including a large block play area. Changing displays make this museum a place to visit over and over again. Spectacular views of the Bay can be had from the large outside observation deck where tikes can climb on several large sculptures, including a whale. A nice museum store is part of the museum's recent renovations.

Food A café is located in the lower level of the building and offers sandwiches, drinks, salads, and desserts.
Strawberry Canyon Swimming Area is just down the hill on Centennial Drive.

Driving Hwy. 24 W to Fish Ranch Road exit. Right onto Fish Ranch Road. Right onto Grizzly Peak Boulevard. Or, 80/580 to University Avenue exit. Left onto Oxford Street. Right onto Hearst Avenue. Right onto Gayley Road. Left onto Centennial Drive.

MOCHA - Museum of Children's Art

Oakland—538 9th Street
(510) 465–8770 / www.mocha.org

Hours: 10:00 a.m. to 5:30 p.m. Tuesday through Friday
10:00 a.m. to 5:00 p.m. Saturday
12:00 p.m. to 5:00 p.m. Sunday

Fee: Free

The MOCHA gallery showcases art created by children from the Bay Area and beyond. The Museum also hosts Open Studios, daily drop-in art programs for kids and their families. The Big Studio is for those 6 years and older and offers guided art projects Tuesday through Friday 3:30 p.m. to 5:00 p.m. and Saturday and Sunday from 1:00 p.m. to 4:00

East Bay

p.m. The Little Studio is focused on providing unstructured art fun for those 18 months to 5 years and is open Tuesday through Sunday 11:00 a.m. to 2:00 p.m. Both studios are $3 per registrant or free for members. MOCHA also offers a variety of classes, workshops, and camps.

Museum is near Oakland's downtown area, Chinatown, and Jack London Square.   **Food**

I-880 S to Union Street exit. Continue on Union Street. Right onto 7th Street. Left   **Driving**
onto Clay Street. Right onto 9th Street.

Oakland Museum

Oakland—1000 Oak St./10th Street
(510) 238–2200 / www.museumca.org

East Bay

Hours: 10:00 a.m. to 5:00 p.m. Wednesday through Saturday
12:00 p.m. to 5:00 p.m. Sunday
First Friday of the month open until 9:00 p.m.

Fee: Adults $6.00, Youth $4.00, Under 5 free
Second Sunday of every month free.

A combination of natural sciences, history, and art, the Oakland Museum is a great rainy day destination. The natural science gallery is particularly good for inquisitive youngsters, with many dioramas displaying much of California's physical wealth. The history gallery is also very good, but curious hands might have a hard time not touching some of the inviting displays. Don't miss the art gallery and be sure to check on any special exhibits. The museum is okay for all ages, but best for toddlers and older.

The museum has a café overlooking a koi pond.

Fairyland is close by at the Lake in the center of town.   **Make a Day**

I-880 N to Oak Street exit. Right onto Oak Street. Or, I-580 E to I-980 W to   **Driving**
Jackson Street exit. Left onto Oak Street.

Water Play: Beaches, Lakes, Pools, & Boating

East Bay

Antioch Water Park
Antioch—4701 Lone Tree Way
(925) 776–3070 / www.ci.antioch.ca.us

Hours: May through Labor Day—12:00 p.m. to 8:00 p.m. Daily
September—11:00 a.m. to 7:00 p.m. Sunday through Friday
11:00 a.m. to 6:00 p.m. Saturday

Fee: $6.00 Monday through Friday, $8.00 Saturday and Sunday,
Under 2 free with paying adult.
After 4:00 p.m. is $4.00

This clean, safety-conscious facility gets rave reviews. Its five pools include a large wading pool that is great for toddlers and five water slides for guests of various abilities. Adventurous kids under four feet tall can also enjoy the Otter Slide or can don a life vest (provided by the park) to ride Humphrey's Slide, Crystal Slide, and Rattler's Run. The Canyon Run slide is reserved for guests taller than four feet. Tadpool drop-in on select mornings—nominal fee and use for 2 hours. Wading pool for little kids.

Arrive early to grab one of the few shady spots in the park. The facility does not allow outside food or beverages into the park and bags are checked upon entry. Swim lessons are available and begin with 6 month-olds.

Food The park includes a snack bar and picnic tables are located before the entrance at the end of the parking lot, plus there are several shopping malls and fast food concessions along Lone Tree Way.

Driving I-680 N to Hwy 4 Lone Tree Exit

Clarke Memorial Swim Center in Heather Farm Park
Walnut Creek—1750 Heather Drive
(925) 943–5856 / www.ci.walnut-creek.ca.us

Hours: 12:00 p.m. to 4:00 p.m Saturday and Sunday (recreational swim hours)

Fee: Adults (16+) $3.50, Youth (7–15) $3.00, Child (6 & Under) $2.25
Family Summer Pass Fee: $200 (good for Larkey Swim Center too)

A guaranteed cool dip in hot weather, this swim center has a great kiddie (two to three and a half feet deep) pool as well as a large lap pool. The pool is heated to 80 degrees with certified lifeguards. Swim lessons April through October for thoe 3 years and older.

There is a snack bar in the swim center.   **Food**

Located next to Heather Farm (see review) with playground, duck ponds, and garden center.   **Make a Day**

I-680 N towards Ygnacio Valley Road. Right onto Ygnacio Valley Road. Left onto N. San Carlos Drive.   **Driving**

Contra Loma Reservoir

Antioch—1200 Frederickson Lane
(925) 757-0404 / www.ebparks.org

Hours: Memorial Day to Labor Day—11:00 a.m. to 6:00 p.m Daily
Other months—11:00 a.m. to 6:00 p.m. Weekends
Closed November through March

Fee: Adult $3.00, Children $1.50
Parking fee $4.00

Control Loma Reservoir opened a fabulous new swimming lagoon May 2002. This lagoon has a sandy beach entrance but then changes to a regular swimming pool bottom. The water is very clear, so little ones can see to the bottom—five feet at its deepest. The water is filtered and chlorinated. Only the toilet-trained are allowed in the lagoon. Lifeguards are on duty during all open hours.

There is a refreshment stand at lake.   **Food**

From Contra Loma there are trail connections to Black Diamond Mines Regional Preserve (see review).   **Make a Day**

Hwy 4 to Lone Tree Way exit. Right onto Golf Course Road. Right onto Frederickson Lane.   **Driving**

Crown Memorial State Beach and Crab Cove Visitor Center

Alameda—1252 MacKay Avenue
(510) 521-6887 / www.ebparks.org

Hours: Visitors Center—March through November—Wednesdays through Sundays

Fee: Parking $4.00

Crown Beach is a small rocky beach with interesting tide pools. It is part of a designated California estuarine marine reserve and an important wildlife habitat. It is best for toddlers and older. A bike/stroller path

East Bay

takes you to an adjacent long stretch of protected sandy beach-perfect for wading. There are no lifeguards on duty. At the Crab Cove Visitor Center, you can see live undersea creatures, plunge into San Francisco Bay without getting wet, or travel back in time to Alameda's colorful past, and picnic on the lawn area. The visitors center is undergoing a renovation which sould be complete spring 2003.

Food A number of fast food places and small grocery stores line Webster Street as you come in from Oakland.

Driving CA-260 S to Central Avenue exit. Right onto Central Avenue. Left onto McKay Avenue.

Don Castro Lake
Hayward—22400 Woodroe Avenue
(510) 538-1148 / www.ebparks.org

Hours: Memorial Day to Labor Day—11:00 a.m. to 6:00 p.m Daily
Other months—11:00 a.m. to 6:00 p.m. Weekends
Closed November through March

Fee: Parking $4.00 Weekends and Holidays
Lagoon—Adults (17+) $2.50, Youth $1.50

The clear blue waters of the Don Castro swim lagoon are beautiful and provide a great getaway destination. The sandy beach has a large shallow area that is roped off especially for children. The adjacent lake is closed to boating and swimming, but trails along the shore take hikers to a miniature wilderness, where turtles and frogs splash in the water, ducks rest in the reeds and raccoons and deer come down to drink at sunset.

Food A snack bar and large lawn areas with picnic sites are nearby.

Driving I-580 E to Center Street/Crow Canyon Road exit. Right onto Center Street. Left onto Kelly Street. Left onto Woodroe Avenue.

Lafayette Reservoir
Lafayette—Mt Diablo Boulevard
(925) 284–9669 / www.lafayettereservoir.com

Fee: Parking $5.00 inside Lafayette Reservoir or 50¢ per half-hour in metered parking

Lafayette Reservoir is a recreation area that is great for hiking, fishing, and boating. Toddlers and older will enjoy the pedal boats and rowboats that can be rented for $15.00 an hour, $25.00 half-day, or $35.00 full

East Bay

day. Life vests are provided. A deposit of $30.00 is required. Familes can rent a boat and stop along the shore somewhere to have lunch at one of the 125 picnic tables located throughout the reservoir.

Lafayette Reservoir can be a whole day event. In addition to renting boats, families can visit the two small, older wooden play structures located on each end of parking lot near the picnic areas, or take a walk on the Lafayette Reservoir Trail (see review).

Food

You'll need to bring food and picnic supplies into the park. You can grab some food at the numerous coffee shops, grocery stores, and fast food restaurants located along Mt. Diablo Boulevard in Lafayette.

Driving

Hwy 24 to Acalanes Road. Head to Mt. Diablo Boulevard.

Lake Anza

Albany—Tilden Regional Park off Canon and Wildcat Canyon Rd
(510) 562-7275 / www.ebparks.org

East Bay

Hours: Spring through October—11:00 a.m. to 6:00 p.m. Daily

Fee: Adult (16–61) $3.00, Child (1–15) $2.50

This is a favorite destination for many East Bay residents. Swimming in the lake, however, is limited to adults and toilet-trained kids. The beach and lawn areas are fun for romping, particularly after a visit to the nearby Little Farm and Environmental Education Center (see review). Lifeguards are on duty 11:00 a.m. to 6:00 p.m. but swimming is allowed at your own risk outside of those hours.

Driving

I-80 E/I-580 W to Gilman Street exit. Right onto Gilman Street. Left onto Hopkins Street. Left onto Sutter Street. Right onto Del Norte Street. Bear right onto the Cir. Right onto Marin Avenue. Left onto Grizzly Peak Boulevard. Right onto Sunset Lane. Right onto Wildcat Canyon Road.

Lake Temescal

Oakland—6500 Broadway Terrace
(510) 652-1155 / www.ebparks.org

Hours: Memorial Day to Labor Day—11:00 a.m. to 6:00 p.m Daily
Other months—11:00 a.m. to 6:00 p.m. Weekends
Closed November through March

Fee: Parking fee $4.00 weekends and holidays
Swimming—Adults (18+) $2.50, Under 17 $1.50

Lake Temescal (cont)

This 10-acre lake has a sandy swim beach. It does get a little chilly in the mornings, but is nice and warm the later part of the day. Only adults or toilet-trained kids are allowed in the water. Lifeguards are on duty during the hours listed above, but there is swim at your own risk when lifeguards are not on duty. The park has picnic and barbeque areas.

Fishing is allowed year-round in this well-stocked lake. Children under 17 do not require a fishing license. There are two children play areas—one in the north and one in the south.

Driving CA-13 S to Broadway Terrace exit. Bear right onto Broadway Terrace.

Larkey Park Swim Center

Walnut Creek—2771 Buena Vista Avenue at First Avenue
(925) 939–1532 / www.ci.walnut-creek.ca.us

Hours: Memorial Day to Labor Day—11:00 a.m. to 6:00 p.m Daily
Other months—11:00 a.m. to 6:00 p.m. Weekends
Closed November through March

Fee: Adults (16+) $3.00, Youth (7–15) $2.50, Children 6 & Under $1.75
Family Summer Pass Fee: $155 (good for Clarke Swim Center)

The Larkey Park Swim Center has a lap pool and a fenced wading pool that is one-foot deep. The swim center is in Larkey Park, which includes two playgrounds (see review) and is next to the Lindsay Wildlife Museum (see review).

Food Larkey Park also has picnic areas, and food can be obtained in nearby Walnut Creek. The nearest food is along North Main Street.

Driving Hwy 24 to North Pleasant Hill Road exit. Continue on Pleasant Hill. Continue straight on Geary. Turn right onto Buena Vista.

Olympic Pool and Aquatic Center

San Ramon—9900 Broadmoor Drive
(925) 973–3240 / www.ci.san-ramon.ca.us

Hours: Father's Day through Labor Day 11:00 a.m. to 6:00 p.m. Daily
Outside of that time 12:00 p.m. to 5:00 p.m. Weekends
Closed November through March.

Fee: Adult (18+) $2.25, Youth (7–17) $1.75, Child (1-6) $1.25
Family passes available $100 for residents and $125 for non-residents

East Bay

This wonderful outdoor 50-meter pool is kept at 80 degrees year-round and includes a water slide, zero depth play area, and inner tube zone. Olympic Pool and Aquatic Center hosts a large array of swim classes starting for children 1.5 years. Call for more information.

I-580 E to Foothill Road/San Ramon Road. Continue on Foothill Road/San Ramon **Driving**
Road. Continue on San Ramon Valley Road. Right onto Pine Valley Road. Left onto Broadmoor Drive.

Pleasant Hill Park Pool
Pleasant Hill—147 Gregory Lane
(925) 682-7830 / www.pleasanthillrec.com

Hours: 1:30 p.m. to 4:30 p.m. Monday through Friday
1:00 p.m. to 6:30 p.m. Saturday
1:00 p.m. to 4:30 p.m. Sunday

Fee: Adult (18+) $2.50, Youth (7–17) $2.25, Child (Under age 6) $1.25

The pool complex includes a fenced wading pool, as well as a lap pool. It is part of the Pleasant Hill Park which also includes a great children's play structure, picnic/barbeque areas, and sports fields.

Snacks and shops in nearby Pleasant Hill Shopping District, including **Food**
Borders and Michaels Art Store.

I-680 N to Contra Costa Boulevard exit. Left onto Gregory Lane. **Driving**

Prewett Family Water Park and Community Center
See Antioch Water Park

Roberts Pool
Oakland—Roberts Regional Recreation Area, 11500 Skyline Boulevard
(510) 636-1684 / www.ebparks.org

Hours: May through September—Daily. Call for specific hours.

Fee: Adult (16–61) $2.50, Child (1–15) $1.50, Under 1 year free

The Roberts Pool complex features a 25-yard, heated swimming pool with a depth of 3 feet to 8.5 feet (no diving board). The park also includes a children's play area, playing fields, and picnic areas. The entrance to the park is in a lovely grove of redwoods. Swimming lessons are available for those 3 and older.

East Bay

Make a Day In the vicinity of Chabot Space and Science Center (see review).
Driving I-580 E to 35th Avenue exit. Left onto 35th Avenue. Continue on Redwood Drive. Left onto Skyline Boulevard.

Soda Aquatics Center

Morago—At Campolindo High School, 300 Moraga Rd
(925) 376–6597 / www.acalanes.k12.ca.us

Hours: Contact for recreational swim hours.

Fee: Adult (18–59) $3.00, Youth (17 and under) $2.00

This new facility houses three pools that are kept exceptionally clean and maintained at a temperature of at least 80 degrees. Although it is part of the Campolindo High School, it is open to the public. Note that there is not a toddler pool. Swim lessons are available and start for those 6 months of age.
Food and other shops in nearby Rheem Shopping Center.
CA-24 E to Camino Pablo exit. Right onto Camino Pablo. Continue on Moraga Way. Left onto Moraga Road. Left onto Campolindo Drive.

Strawberry Canyon Recreation Area

Berkeley—East of the main UC Berkeley Campus on Centennial Drive
(510) 643–6720 / www.strawberry.org/swim

Hours: 12:00 p.m. to 6:00 p.m. Weekdays
11:00 a.m. to 6:00 p.m. Weekends except on UC-Berkeley football game days.
Closed November to April.

Fee: Adults $5.00, Children (Under 16) $ 3.00

The SCRA is open to all members of the community, without regard to UC affiliation. The West Pool is a great place to enjoy a swim (water wings are allowed) or you can wade and splash in the kiddie pool. Berkeley can be foggy during the summer so be sure to check the weather before driving over. The web site has a weather cam.
Food There is a nice lawn area for eating/relaxing, but the only food source—vending machines—provide a limited selection of snack food. On the way to Lawrence Hall of Science.
Driving I-80 to the University Ave. exit. Proceed east on University Ave. to the western edge of campus at Oxford At Oxford turn left and go to Hearst Ave. Turn right and head up the hill on Hearst. Go all the way up to Gayley Rd. Make a right on Gayley.

East Bay

Proceed past the Greek Theatre on your right to Stadium Rim Way. Turn left on
Stadium Rim Way and proceed up to the stop sign. (The Memorial Stadium will be
on your right) Turn left on to Centennial Dr. Go approximately 100 yards and you
will see a parking lot on the right. The entrance to the Haas Clubhouse is on the
far southeast end of the lot. OR, exit at Ashby Ave. (Highway 13) into Berkeley.
Proceed on Ashby to College Ave. and turn right Go to Dwight Way and turn right
Go up hill to Prospect and turn left Proceed around the stadium (to your left) to the
first "Stop" sign Turn right onto Centennial Dr. Go approximately 100 yds and the
SCRA Parking Lot is on your right.

East Bay

Out and About: Hikes, Bikes & Stroller Trails

Black Diamond Mines Regional Preserve
Antioch—5175 Somersville Rd.
(925) 757-2620 / www.ebparks.org

Hours: Preserve—daily
Visitor Center—March through November—10:00 a.m. to 4:30 p.m. Weekends

Fee: Parking $4.00 Weekends March through November

Black Diamond Mines Regional Preserve was the site of a 19th century coal mine and three towns. This 5,700-acre preserve now contains 47 miles of trails that let you view the hill-covered wildflowers in the spring, explore the ruins of the mining towns, and take a look at the Rose Hill Cemetery where many of the long ago inhabitants of the coal mining towns were buried. The trails meander throughout the reserver, letting you select the best terrain and length for your children.
Hwy 4 to Somersville Road exit. South (toward the hills) on Somersville Road.

Coyote Hills Regional Park
Fremont—8000 Patterson Ranch Rd
(510) 795-9385 / www.ebparks.org

Fee: Parking $4.00

This 976-acre park located on Fremont Bay's shoreline includes the Bay View Trail, a 3.5 mile paved bike/hike trail that loops around this wildlife sanctuary and offers some great views. The Visitors Center, open 9:30 a.m. to 5:00 p.m. Tuesday through Sunday, includes exhibits on Native Americans, the East Bay's original inhabitants.

Driving Hwy 84 W to Paseo Padre Parkway exit. North on Paseo Padre Parkway. Left onto Patterson Ranch Road (parking fee).

Inspiration Point—Nimitz Trail
Berkeley—Tilden Regional Park, Wildcat Canyon entry
(510) 525-2233 / www.ebparks.org

This very wide, four-mile paved and gravel path is greal for all ages, including children in strollers and young walkers. It winds along the top

East Bay

of Tilden Regional Park offering spectacular views of the Bay, reservoirs, and Mt Diablo. The path is gently hilly.

Stop in Orinda Village for refreshments or supplies and have a picnic at Inspiration Point.   **Food**

Little Train, Little Farm and other Tilden Regional Park destinations are within a 10-minute drive.   **Make a Day**

Enter the park from its east side from Wildcat Canyon Road off Camino Pablo just north of Orinda Village (take the Orinda exit off Highway 24 east of the Caldecott Tunnel).   **Driving**

Iron Horse Regional Trail
Walnut Creek to Danville—Newell and Broadway in Walnut Creek or at Rudgear and I-680 at Walnut Creek
(925) 687-3419 / www.ebparks.org

The Iron Horse Regional Trail will eventually cover 33 miles (currently covers 12.5 miles), connecting Livermore to Suisun Bay—all paved. The best part of the trail is the portion from Walnut Creek to Danville. It makes a nice stroll for parents with kids in strollers and a pleasant walk for walking tots and preschoolers. Portions of the existing trail will be closed during 2003/2004. Call (925) 935-6049 for details.

Broadway Plaza Shopping near Newell has many amenities including coffee shops and Whole Foods Market is close by,   **Food**

Lafayette-Moraga Trail
Lafayette and Moraga—Olympic Boulevard/Pleasant Hill Rd; St. Mary's Road/ Moraga Road
(510) 562-7275 / www.ebparks.org

This 60-foot-wide, flat and paved trail extends from Pleasant Hill Road to Moraga Commons—approximately six miles—and continues another mile to the Valle Vista Staing Area on Canyon Road. The trail from Pleasant Hill Road to Moraga Commons is the best for kids in strollers, walkers, and young bikers. It winds through pasturelands and behind wooded suburbs along an old railroad grade. When you get to Moraga Commons, you can enjoy the playground, access bathrooms, and grab some food at the Moraga Shopping Center.

East Bay

Lafayette Reservoir Trail

Lafayette—Mt Diablo Boulevard
(925) 284–9669 / www.lafayettereservoir.com

Fee: Parking $5.00 inside Lafayette Reservoir;
50¢ per half-hour in metered parking (two-hour limit)

The Lafeyette Reservoir trail is a gentle three-mile walk around Lafayette Reservoir. This wide, paved 2.7-mile trail is slightly hilly but is doable for strollers and young children. Ten outhouses are staged along the trail. Bicycles and rollerblades are allowed on the trail Tuesday/Thursday afternoons from noon until closing and Sunday mornings until 11:00 a.m.

You'll need to bring food and picnic supplies into the park. You can grab some food at the numerous coffee shops, grocery stores, and fast food restaurants located along Mt. Diablo Boulevard in Lafayette.

Lafayette Reservoir can be a whole day event. In addition to walking the Lafayette Reservoir Trail, families can visit the two small, older wooden play structures located on each end of parking lot near the picnic areas, or rent a pedal boat or rowboat (see review).

Driving   Acalanes Road exit off Hwy 24 to Mt. Diablo Blvd

Mt Diablo State Park

Clayton and Danville
(925) 837–2525 / www.mdia.org and www.parks.ca.gov

Hours: Visitor Center—Summer—11:00 a.m. to 5:00 p.m. Wednesday through Sunday
Winter—10:00 a.m. to 4:00 p.m.

Fee: $2.00 per car

Majestic Mt Diablo towers over the East Bay and is a preserve of diverse wildlife and distinctive geology. The park has picnic areas, camping sites, and numerous trails. The Fire Interpretive Trail is a .7-mile, fairly flat but narrow trail that encircles the summit of Mt. Diablo. The first one-third of the trail is paved. Other trails are fairly steep, but many can be done with a jog stroller. Most trails require steady walking skills or a jog stroller. The park's Summit Visitor Center has quality exhibits and information on the parks geology, plant and animal life and cultural history that even young children will enjoy. On a clear day, you'll have an uninterrupted view to the Farallons, Mt Shasta, and Half Dome in Yosemite!

Driving   South entrance—Hwy 680 to Danville, take Diablo Road exit, then 3 miles east to

East Bay

Mt. Diablo Scenic Boulevard. North entrance—Hwy 680 to Walnut Creek, take
Ygnacio Valley Rd exit, right onto Walnut Avenue (turns into North Gate Road).

Sibley Volcanic Regional Preserve
Oakland—6800 Skyline Blvd.
www.ebparks.org

This open space is fairly barren but offers some fascinating peaks at
volcanoes. In fact, the Round Top peak is make up of lava and volcanic
debris left over from a 10-million-year-old volcanoe. An easy 2+ mile
hike on the Volcanic Trail—Round Top trail brings you to one of the
highest in the Oakland hills. During the spring, wildflowers cover the
area. This isn't a trail for unstable walkers. Infants and toddlers will need
to ride in backpacks or jog strollers. An unstaffed visitor center at the
entrance displays the park's geology and provides park brochures with a
map of the self-guided volcanic tour.
Hwy 24 to Fish Ranch Road exit. Left onto Skyline Boulevard.

East Bay

Amusements

Baby Brigade

Oakland—Parkway Theater, 1834 Park Boulevard
(510) 814–2400 / www.picturepubpizza.com

Hours: Monday. Showtimes at 6:30 p.m. and 7:00 p.m.

Fee: Adults $5.00

The Parkway Theater is the only spot in the Bay Area where you can order dinner, sit back in a comfy loveseat, and watch a movie on a real screen. Most of the time this theater is for those 21 and over. However, they open their doors to infants 1 year and younger (and their caregivers!) on Monday nights and called it the Baby Brigade. The box office opens 45 minutes before show time. The movie schedule is posted weekly and can be found on the Parkway Theater web site.
I-580 East to Park Boulevard exit. West on Park Boulevard.

Children's Fairyland

Oakland—699 Bellevue Avenue/Grand Avenue
(510) 238–6876 / www.fairyland.org

Hours: Summer—10:00 a.m. to 4:00 p.m. Monday through Friday
10:00 a.m. to 5:00 p.m. Weekends and Holidays
Spring & Fall–10:00 a.m. to 4:00 p.m. Wednesday through Sunday and Holidays
Winter—10:00 a.m. to 4:00 p.m. Friday through Sunday and Holidays

Fee: Unlimited rides $6.00, Under 1 free
Parking $2.00

Once upon a time (in 1950), William Russell Everett designed Children's Fairyland as a simple place for kids to see classic stories brought to life with animals helping to act the stories out. Located in the middle of Lake Merritt Park, the modest 10-acre park was the inspiration for Walt Disney to create a grander version a few years later. Before 2001, aging Fairyland was slowly reverting to pumpkin state, but a renovation has done wonders for the place. Walk through the entrance and the first thing you'll see is a town of donkeys, rabbits, and other critters. As before, much of the park is devoted to small sets in which animals star as storybook characters, with electronic readers (a $2 magic key activates all the readers in the park) reciting the familiar tales to eager tots. Rides include a brand-new carousel, a Ferris wheel, slides, and a mini-train. Kids can ride as often as they like while weary adults can head for benches that form a lounge area. When it's time to wind down, puppeteers and stage shows are within strolling distance and offered at 11:00 a.m., 2:00 p.m., and 4:00 p.m.

Grab a bite at the renovated Johnny Appleseed Café where you can get a burger and coke for under $5.00. **Food**

Lake Merritt is within walking distance, as well as a recently renovated playground adjacent to the lake and a small nature center. **Make a Day**

I-580 E to Harrison Street exit. Right onto Harrison. Left onto Grand Avenue. Or, I-580 W to MacArthur/Harrison Street exit. Left onto Harrison. Left onto Grand Avenue. **Driving**

Pixieland Amusement Park

Concord—Willow Pass Park, 2740 East Olivera Rd
(925) 689–8841 / www.Pixieland.com

East Bay

Hours: Winter—10:00 a.m. to 4:00 p.m. Saturday and Sunday
Spring, Summer, Fall—Contact for days and hours
Closed January

Fee: Admission is free,
Ride tickets $1.25 each
Day Pass $12.00 (available on weekdays, excluding holidays)
Season Pass $80.00

This small amusement park has rides including a tiny train, model-T cars, a carousel, and tea-cups. Pixieland is located adjacent to a duck pond, around which the little train circles. The staff are friendly and helpful. Lines are short if you go during weekday mornings. The park is small and fun to walk for toddlers.

A concession stand inside the park offers standard park fare (corn dogs, popcorn, drinks, etc). **Food**

Hwy 242 E to Olivera Road exit. Right onto Olivera Road. Or, CA-4 W to Willow Pass Road exit. Left onto Willow Pass Road. Right onto Olivera Road. **Driving**

Small World Park

Pittsburg—2551 Harbor St. / Leland
(925) 439–4879

Hours: 11:00 a.m. to 5:00 p.m. Saturdays and Sundays

Fee: Adults $3.50, Children (1–14) $1.75, Under 1 free

This is a seasonal park geared towards families and includes carousel and train rides, streams and ponds (including fishing for crawdads!), as well as play equipment and picnic areas.

Driving   CA-4 E to Railroad Avenue exit. Contine on Railroad Avenue. Left onto E Leland Road. Right onto Harbor Street.

East Bay

Trains, Planes & Automobiles

Blackhawk Automotive Museum

Danville—3700 Blackhawk Plaza Circle
736.2277 / www.blackhawkauto.org

Hours: 10:00 a.m. to 5:00 p.m. Wednesday through Sunday & Holidays on Mondays
Closed Thanksgiving Day, Christmas Day, and New Year's Day

Fee: Adults $8.00; Under 7 free
Family Memberhsip $59.00

The Blackhawk Museum displays rare classic cars, including K. Behring's $100+ million collection. However, the museum is not limited to automotives. It also includes a Smithsonian Gallery and Natural History Gallery where traveling Smithsonian exhibitions are often hosted. The museum is best for preschoolers and older but is of interest to car fanatics of all ages.

There are several places to eat in the Blackhawk Shopping Center.

I-680 to Crow Canyon Road. East to Camino Tassajara. Right onto Camino Tassajara. Left onto Blackhawk Plaza Circle.   **Driving**

East Bay

Golden Gate Live Steamers

Berkeley—Grizzly Peak Blvd
(510) 486-0623 / www.ggls.org

Hours: 12:00 p.m. to 3:00 p.m. Sunday, weather permitting

Fee: Donations appreciated

GGSL offers rides on miniature steam trains that are operated by club members. These are smaller trains than those operated by Redwood Valley Railway (see review). This is best for toddlers and older, as children need to be able to hold onto the long bench seat.

Hwy 80 to Albany exit. Right onto Marin Avenue. Continue on Marin. Left onto Grizzly Peak.   **Driving**

Golden State Model Railroad Museum

Pt. Richmond—900A Dornan Drive
(510) 234-4884 / www.gsmrm.org

Hours: April through December—12:00 p.m. to 5:00 p.m. Saturdays and Sundays
Open Memorial Day, July 4, and Labor Day

Fee: Adults $3.00, Under 12 $2.00, Families $7.00

The East Bay Model Engineers Society operates three model train layouts that occupy more than 10,000 square feet. This is best for toddlers and older.
I-580 to Canal Boulevard exit. Right at the stop sign. Left onto Garrard Boulevard. Continue on Dornan Drive.

Horse-Drawn Railroad at Ardenwood Historic Farm

Fremont—34600 Ardenwood Blvd.

The railroad is run by the Society for Preservation of Carter Railroad Resources and is located on the historic Ardenwood Farm (see review). The 1-mile ride is powered by draft horses, making this the only regularly scheduled horse-drawn railroad in the United States.

Little Train/Redwood Valley Rail Corp.

Berkeley—Tilden Regional Park, Grizzly Peak Blvd. & Lomas Cantadas
(510) 548-6100 / www.redwoodvalleyrailway.com

Hours: Year Round—11:00 a.m. to 6:00 p.m. Weekends & Holidays
Summer—12:00 a.m. to 5:00 p.m. Weekdays and Easter
Closed Thanksgiving and Christmas Day

Fee: Single ride $1.75, Five ticket ride $7.00, Under 2 free

The train ride is about 12 minutes long, and leaves every 15-20 minutes. The train offers small-scale open and covered cars that pass through the redwoods, over a trestle, through a tunnel, and around many curves. The operation recreates an old-time narrow gauge atmosphere with authentically designed locomotives, wooden cars and scale buildings. You can also head down the hill to Golden Gate Live Steamers for free rides on smaller steam trains (see review).

East Bay

Follow signs to get to Little Farm, Pony Rides and Carousel (see review), located at the northern end of park.

Westbound/Eastbound on 24. Exit at Fish Ranch Road, near the Caldecott Tunnel. **Driving**
Turn right at the T, uphill on Fish Ranch Rd. At the 4-way, ridgetop intersection, turn right on Grizzly Peak Blvd. Go 1 winding mile, taking the first right onto Lomas Cantadas Rd., then immediately turn left, and left again to enter our parking area.

Niles Canyon Railway
Sunol—Sunol Depot at 6 Kilkare Rd.
(925) 862–9063 / www.ncry.org

Hours: May through September on first, second, and third Sunday
October through March on first and third Sunday
First train departs at 10:30 a.m. and last train departs at 3:00 p.m.

Fee: Suggested donation: Adults $8.00; Children (3-12) $4.00, Under 2 free

The Niles Canyon Railroad is something kids of all ages are sure to enjoy but is best for toddlers. The railway runs along the last remnant of Central Pacific line, part of the transcontinental railway built in the 1860s that once wound through Stockton, Altamont Pass, Livermore and Niles Canyon to Oakland. Both a steam train and a skunk train depart for a 12-mile round trip (about an hour) from Sunol to Niles Canyon. All trains have open cars, covered cars, and enclosed coaches, so be sure to dress appropriately.

Some food is available at the market across the street from the depot. **Food**
Nothing is available on train, so come prepared.

I-880 Fremont. Decoto Road exit. Northeast to Alvarado-Niles Blvd. Right onto **Driving**
Niles Blvd. Cross Mission Blvd. onto Hwy 84/Niles Canyon Rd. Continue to the Sunol exit

East Bay

Oakland Zoo Train
Oakland —
(510) 632–9523 / www.oaklandzoo.org

Entrance Fee: Train: $1.50 (2 ride tickets) for all over 2 years

The train ride (located in a small amusement park near the entrance of the zoo) runs through the zoo and along a ridge with a terrific view of the Bay. Other rides in the amusement park are geared towards toddlers and preschoolers. See Oakland Zoo entry (see review).

Western Aerospace Museum
Oakland—8260 Boeing St., Bldg. #621
(510) 638–7100 / www.westernaerospacemuseum.org

East Bay

Hours: 10:00 a.m. to 4:00 p.m. Wednesday through Sunday

Fee: Adults $7.00, Youth (6–12) $5.00, Under 6 free

Historic aircraft, as well as some modern Navy jet fighters, are on display in an authentic hangar. The exhibit rooms include flying memorabilia and photographs. The museum is best for well-behaved preschoolers and older who have shown an interest in aviation.

Driving   I-880 to Oakland Airport/Hegenberger Rd exit. Follow signs to the Oakland Airport past Doolittle Dr (Hilton Hotel). Turn left at first red light and then an immediate right onto Earhart Rd and drive 0.7 miles. When Hanger #6 is on your left (Alaska Airlines), take next right and you'll see parking lot and signs.

Teaching Our Children to Play Well With Others

Over the past four years, I've attended parenting classes at "Resources for Infant Educators" (RIE) with renowned child therapist Magda Gerber. Gerber, now 80 years old, founded RIE in 1978 to share with parents and child care professionals insights she gained while working with hundreds of orphans in her native Hungary at the end of Word War II. Gerber, along with her small staff, teaches vital parenting skills that respect a child's individuality. RIE encourages parents to raise emotionally-intelligent (not just intellectually driven) children capable of authentic, healthy self-expression.

Gerber stress that a paramount step in an individual's journey to authentic self-expression is emotional self-awareness. The child develops this emotional awareness, in part, during conflicts with other children. RIE offers parents what might be surprising advice on encouraging children to play "well" with others - "Do less and observe more."

"Doing less and observing more" warns pushy parents, who would otherwise rush in to solve their children's conflicts, to back off and give the child space to develop and express their individual preferences. Gerber points out that for young children, even negative interactions promote socialization. The child learns, for example, that bullying evokes a negative response from a playmate or that yelling discourages interaction. In other words, the child draws a connection between their behavior and their peers' responses. The child then adjusts his or her behavior accordingly and so begins the process of learning how to play "nicely." No amount of lecturing can substitute for these lessons learned during actual interactions with other children.

Children capable of playing well with others have developed their skills over time. Sharing is virtually incomprehensible to a child under four. "Taking turns" is equally baffling for young children -- i.e., how long is my turn supposed to be? Nevertheless, children are more likely to arrive at a workable solution if given the time and opportunity.

RIE offers the following approach when children are in conflict -- move in close but, do not interrupt the conflict, tell the children in non-judgmental language that you are watching and that you are going to ensure that neither child is physically harmed (e.g. " I see you both want the shovel. I'm not going to allow hitting.") and let the children work it out. Be warned, however. When young children work it out there will often be a winner and a loser. So, first, we as parents must learn not to over-invest emotionally in the outcome of children's disputes. RIE does not allow any child to physically harm another, but it does allow the fastest to out pace the slowest, the loudest to out yell the quietest, and the strongest to overpower the weaker. Winning and losing is allowed as means to an end. What is the end? -- raising children that can cope with both negative and positive interactions and who can express their emotions in a healthy way. By interfering less frequently, we communicate a powerful esteem-enhancing message to our children - "I respect you and whatever you two can come up with can work." Even when working through negative interactions our children learn what it takes to play well with others. As parents seeking to raise well-liked children, we should remember that conflicts are often important opportunities for our children to grow. By doing so, we help them along the path to being self-aware and emotionally-authentic individuals.

Stacey Bowers, a J.D./M.B.A.,
is a full-time mother of two and Freelance writer.

Selecting a Safe Playground

Since the first public playground was established in Boston, Massachusetts in 1886, public playgrounds have been a popular destination for families. Playgrounds offer so many benefits for children including FUN, exercise, social skills, and confidence. Unfortunately, not all playgrounds are suitable for young children. As a parent, you'll need to evaluate what seems appropriate for the age and personality of your children.

There are sixteen important ingredients that make up an excellent and ideal toddler playground:

1. A fenced-in play area where no animals are allowed
2. Toddler area and equipment are separate from the playground for older children
3. Equipment meets toddlers needs and not just has high aesthetic adult appeal
4. Space between equipment is ample for toddlers to roam from one to another without being hurt
5. Equipment is clean and well maintained with no broken, rusty, damaged, loose, or missing parts
6. Surface of playground has a soft surface made of rubber mats or loose fill like wood mulch or sand, instead of asphalt or concrete
7. Sand area where groups of toddlers can play which according to recent research is the favorite play activity of toddlers
8. Structures are small and designed for toddler's ages 18 months to five-years-old
9. Equipment anchored firmly with devices set below the surface to prevent tripping over them
10. Bucket swings are made of lightweight, impact absorbing materials like plastic or rubber that are placed two to three feet apart to reduce chances of midair collisions
11. Slides are wide and height-appropriate with less than a 30 degree incline and the platform is connected to the slide, with guardrails and rubber mats at end of the slides
12. Low wooden climbing structures/jungle gyms that are no taller than the children who are using them
13. Low steps and beams
14. Tunnels to crawl through
15. Rocking horses
16. Miniature bridge which like all elevated structures is no higher than 20 to 30 inches and includes guardrails

Very few playgrounds will be perfect or have everything, but hopefully you will find one that offers most of the ingredients for an excellent playground.

Elizabeth English, Founder of Parenting Learning Center
www.parentlc.com

Babies are necessary to grown-ups. A new baby is like the beginning of all things --wonder, hope, a dream of possibilities. In a world that is cutting down its trees to build highways, losing its earth to con-crete... babies are almost the only remaining link with nature, with the natural world of living things from which we spring.

Eda J. Le Shan

Parks & Playgrounds

Belvedere Park

Belvedere—San Rafael Avenue / Community Road
(415) 435–4355

North Bay

This is a gated park with clean sand and is appropriate for infants, early walkers, and older. It has a nice play structure that is less than 10 years old. There are three baby swings, three regular swings, a tree house, a seesaw, and a metal fire engine.Benches inside the gate allow you to view your children playing, and picnic tables outside the gate on the grassy area provide you an opportunity for a picnic. There are some shade trees. A basketball court is next to the playground. This park is well worth the drive if you are in Marin.

Driving   Hwy 101 N to Tiburon exit. East to Tiburon. Right onto San Rafael Ave. Left onto Leeward Road. Immediate right onto Community Road.

Blackies Pasture Recreation Area and Playground

Tiburon—Tiburon Boulevard/Blackies Pasture Road
(415) 435–4355

This impressive recreational area offers spectacular views of San Francisco. Two paths, one paved and one of gravel, head into downtown Tiburon along Richardson Bay with benches and water fountains along the way. There are nice easy trail for bikers of all ages and wide enough to tow a Burley bike trailer. A wildlife pond on the north side has ducks and cranes.

Further along the trail, behind a small hill, is the actual park. There is a fenced playground with a slide, infant swing, and boat play structure and an unfenced playground that has a wooden/metal/plastic play structure with a slide, tire swing, two infant swings and a regular swing. Grassy areas surround the play area. The small hill has an unpaved trail leading to the peak and, on a nice day, it is a perfect spot for a picnic (appropriate for older children and infants). It is also the best seat in the park if a soccer game is going on down below on McKegney Field. This is a very nice park, especially on a sunny day. However, it can be cold and windy even on a clear day.

Food   It's an easy ride into Tiburon where you can catch a bite to eat at Guaymas or hop on the ferry to Angel Island.

Driving   Hwy 101N to Tiburon/Hwy 131 exit. Right onto Blackies Pasture Road.

Boyle Park

Mill Valley—E. Blithedale Avenue/East Drive
(415) 383-1370 / www.cityofmillvalley.org

This is a sunny, well-fenced playground with plenty of sand. It includes a wooden/metal/plastic play structure with three slides, four infant swings, a caboose, a hut with a table, and two benches sized for toddlers. Outside the fenced area is a recently installed metal/wooden play structure with two swings for older children and recently added infant swings, a slide, and rings. A metal fence on the perimeter of the park closest to the play area prevents kids from rolling down the embankment into the creek.

Adjacent to the play area is a grassy park with picnic benches/tables around the perimeter shaded by trees. Next door is a baseball field and four tennis courts.

Hwy 101 to E. Blithedale/Tiburon exit. Right on East Drive. **Driving**

Dolliver Park

Larkspur—Magnolia Avenue/ Madrone
(415) 927-6746

This well-shaded park is ideal for those stiflingly hot days, hence the nickname Dark Park. It consists of several older structures underlain by dirt and sand. The playground includes old fashioned swings, climbing structures, merry go round, and a very tall, scary tornado slide. The slide can be frightening for kids and parents. The slide and any structure underlain by dirt can be dangerous. The playground is best for preschoolers and older. There is a creek behind the park that is fun to explore, but keep an eye on your kids. Note: There are rumors that this park will soon be renovated but some neighbors reportedly want to keep some of the older structures for nostalgic purposes.

Hwy 101 N to Tamalpais Drive/Paradise Drive exit. Left onto Tamalpais **Driving** Drive. Left onto Redwood Avenue. Right onto Corte Madera. Continue onto Magnolia Avenue.

Freitas Memorial Park

San Rafael—Montecillo Road at Trellis Drive
(415) 485-3333

This park has been nicely landscaped with a large grassy area that

North Bay

slopes down toward the waterplay area. The waterplay area has a circular,colored rubberized surface with four red metallic rings forming a tunnel.Water sprays out from inside the rings forming four walls of water. Kids love running through it and coming out soaked at the other end.This is a great park to cool off on those hot summer Marin days. There is only one hut and a few young trees for shade. Because there are no other play structures at this park,when the water is turned off during the cooler months, it does not have much else to offer.

Northgate Mall is about six blocks away and is the closest place to get something to eat.

101 N to Freitas Parkway exit towards Terra Linda. Continue on Manuel T Freitas Parkway. Left onto Las Pavadas Avenue. Left onto Montecillo Road.

Howarth Park

Santa Rosa—650 Summerfield Road/Montomery Drive
(707) 543-3282

Hours: Park—Daily
            Rides—Memorial Day to Labor Day 11:00 a.m. to 5:00 p.m. Daily
            Labor Day through October 11:00 a.m. to 5:00 p.m. Saturday and Sunday

Fees: Park—Free
            Rides—Train and Carousel $1.50 per ride, Petting zoo $2.00, Boats $7.00 hour

Howarth Park is a fabulous destination for a day trip—well worth the hour and 10 minute drive from San Francisco, especially when San Francisco is fogged in! There are a couple of different playground areas. One includes a climbing structure, make-believe old western town, digging area with water, and swings (both for infants and older kids). All includes swings, a slide, and climbing structures. However, the main attractions at Howarth Park are the carousel—smaller and less intimidating to a little child than the ones at the San Francisco Zoo and Yerba Buena Gardens, a miniature train that circles the park, a small petting zoo, and rowboat and pedal boat (707) 543–3425)) rides on the lake. The petting zoo and boats are only available during the summer.

Unfortunately, the park is not fenced and some of the play areas are dangerously close to the parking lot. The lake is only partially fenced. This isn't a big problem if your kids are 3 and up, but if you are bringing younger than that bring one adult per child. The bathrooms are in disrepair—no doors on some.

Food   Food is available but it tends to be pricey and consists mostly of junk food. So, it is best to bring your own picnic.

Driving 101 N to Hwy 12 exit. Head east. Left onto Summerfield Road.

Millennium Playground

San Anselmo—Memorial Park, Veterans Place/San Francisco Boulevard
(415) 258-4645 / www.townofsananselmo.org

This huge and amazing community-built playground was designed by
kids in 2000 and includes a water play area with fountains, a wooden
castle, train, mazes, giant dinosaur, climbing wall, swings, slides, and
sandboxes. It will keep children busy for hours in a safe environment.
There are two sections—one for 1- to 5-year-olds and one for 6- to
10-years-olds. The entire playground is fenced and there is only one
exit. The play structures resemble Marin landmarks such as the Bolinas
Lighthouse, Marin Seminary, Dominican College Roof, and Iron Giant
Gate. The park also has picnic tables, softball fields, tennis courts, and
large a lawn area.

Not shaded very well so be sure to bring sunscreen. Park gets extremely
hot during summer months, so it's best to avoid being there from the
hours of 11:00 a.m. until 3:00 p.m. during that time of year.

Close to downtown shopping area and Safeway.

Food

101 N to San Anselmo exit. West on Sir Francis Drake Boulevard. Right on San
Francisco Boulevard. Right on Veterans Place.

Driving

Old Mill Park

Mill Valley—Throckmorton Avenue/Old Mill
(415) 383–1370 / www.cityofmillvalley.org

This park is set amid a redwood grove and includes nice shaded picnic
areas. The park has one play structure, a couple of infant swings, and a
creek. The sand is dusty and dirty from organic material such as leaves
and tree bark. This is the best place to be on those hot summer days
when everyone is looking for shade. Conversely, it's not a great place for
those cooler days. Remnants of Reed Mill remain in the park, as well as
a red, wooden passenger car on the railway.

101 N to CA-1 N exit towards Mill Valley/Stinson Beach. Continue on
CA-1. Continue on Almonte Boulevard. Continue on Miller Avenue. Left on
Throckmorton Avenue.

Driving

Peacock Gap Park

San Rafael—Peacock Drive/San Pedro Road
(415) 485-3333

North Bay

There are two playground areas—one is a fenced toddler area (for ages 2 to 5) with plastic boat, playhouse, backhoe digger, ride-on horses, and four toddler swings. The second area is for older children and has swings, two large climbing structures with multiple slides, and monkey bars. Large grassy area and picnic tables are found throughout park. It is shaded over playground. Tennis courts and a par course are nearby.

Driving 101 N to Central San Rafael exit. East on 2nd Sreet. Continue on Pt. San Pedro Road. Left on Peacock Drive.

Peri Park
Fairfax—Park Road/Bolinas Road

Peri Park's playground includes older wooden structures underlain by sand. The structures offers places to hide and swings, including a tire swing. There is also a creek outside the fence that kids will love to explore. Peri Park is known for its Bocce courts.
Snacks can be found at Fairfax Coffee Roasters, corner of Bolinas and Center.

Driving Center Avenue into Fairfax. Left onto Bolinas Road. Right onto Park Road.

Piper Park
Larkspur—Doherty Drive/Magnolia Avenue
(415) 927-6746 / www.ci.larkspur.ca.us

The playground in Piper Park includes three newer play structures underlain by sand. It also includes infant swings, regular swings, and a tire swing that provide geat views of Mt. Tam. A toddler slide, a higher slide, a tunnel, and monkey bars round out the playground. The park tends to get very puddly for up to several days after a big storm. This is great fun for kids, but be sure to bring extra clothes and expect to give a bath when you get home. Swings have a view of Mt. Tam! The playground is great for crawlers to preschoolers. Piper Park includes walking paths, sand volleyball courts, horeshoe pits, baseball diamonds, tennis courts, and a marina. The nearby middle school occasionally uses the walking paths.

Food The park has a picnic area with grills. Food can be found at Artisan Bakers on Magnolia and Rulli on Magnolia.

Driving 101 N to Tamalpais Drive/Paradise Drive exit. Left onto Tamalpais. Left onto Redwood Avenue. Right on Corte Madera. Continue on Magnolia Avenue. Right onto Doherty Drive.

Stinson Beach Village Green Playground

Stinson Beach—Camino Del Mar/Arenal
(415) 868–2625

This small, well-fenced playground with views of Mount Tamalpais in the background is in an attractive little park within walking distance of the beach. It has one large wooden, metal, and plastic climbing structure underlain by sand with slides, tunnels, and plenty to climb on. There is also a small wooden playhouse and benches. The park has basketball courts, grassy areas, and benches.

The park is very near the shops (antique, surf and other) and restaurants of Stinson Beach. Pick up groceries (or mediocre pre-made sandwiches) for a picnic at Beckers on Shoreline or snacks at Parkside Cafe across the street. Cross Arenal and then a small pedestrian bridge and you'll find yourself in the beach parking lot complete with picnic tables. See Stinson Beach on review.

Driving Hwy 101 N to CA-1 N exit towards Mill Valley/Stinson Beach. Continue on CA-1.

Town Park

Corte Madera—Tamalpais Drive/Pixley Avenue
(415) 927.5072

Town Park includes two large playgrounds—one new playground, Toddler Town, for younger kids and an older, but renovated, playground for older kids. The playgrounds have lots of structures appropriate for a range of ages and include all the basics. Plus, the park has a town that those on bikes and trikes can bike through. This is a great park to bring tricycles or a bicycle with training wheels due to the riding track around the play area. Or, if your kids are into climbing, they will love the climbing wall. If it's a hot day, they can get wet in the water play area. The play areas are underlain by sand, wood chips, and rubber matting. The park has tennis courts, baseball diamonds, and a recreation center within walking distance. The Neil Cummins school is within walking distance and offers additional playground activities.

Food Food can be found outside of the park in Corte Madera Town Square. The park does have a picnic area with barbecue pits.

Driving Hwy 101 N to Tamalpais Drive/Paradise Drive exit. Left onto Tamalpais Ave. Right onto Pixley Avenue.

North Bay

Animals: Zoos, Farms & Nature Centers

North Bay

The Marine Mammal Center
Sausalito—Marin Headlands, 1065 Fort Cronkhite
(415) 289.7325 / www.tmmc.org

Hours: 10:00 a.m. to 4:00 p.m. Daily
Closed Thanksgiving Day, Christmas Day and New Year's Day

Fees: Donations appreciated

The Marine Mammal Center is the largest marine mammal facility in the world to combine animal rehabilitation with an on-site research lab. Toddlers and preschoolers will enjoy watching the marine mammals (seals, sea lions, dolphins, porpoises, whales, and sea otters) as they recover. The Marine Mammal Center's goal is to treat the animals in a hospital area (open to visitors) and release them back into their native marine environment. Therefore, the animals you see is very dependent upon what animals have come into the Center. Call ahead to find out which ones are at the center.

Driving Hwy 101 N to Alexander Avenue exit. Continue on Sausalito Lateral Road. Bear left onto Bunker Road. Bear leaft onto Fort Cronkhite.

Museums: Art, Science & Hands-on

Bay Area Discovery Museum
Sausalito—East Fort Baker, 557 McReynolds Road
(415) 487–4398 / www.badm.org

Hours: 9:00 a.m. to 4:00 p.m. Tuesday through Friday
10:00 a.m. to 5:00 p.m. Saturday and Sunday
Closed Labor Day, Easter, July 4, Thanksgiving Day, and Christmas Day

Fee: Over 1 $7.00. Under 1 free
$85 membership for four
Second Saturday of each month after 1:00 p.m. is free.

North Bay

This hands-on museum is housed in six former Army barracks with a variety of activities that interest children of all ages–crawlers to preschoolers.

Tot Spot, or Baby Mosh Pit as veterans call it, is specifically designed to awaken the senses of children three years and under. There is a height limit for access - not including parents of course! It is a large padded room for romping and playing. There is a stuffed animal pit and a waterbed-type thing with goldfish swimming above it. It also includes a section with what can best be called a giant shape sorter and large blocks for stacking. There is also a space with a squishy floor and one with a distorted mirror.

There's an outdoor gravel area with shovels, pails, and bulldozers. An old fishing boat, a modern speedboat, and an old automobile allow children to climb in and explore.

The Art Spot allows children to use different mediums such as paint, chalk, paper, cardboard, modeling clay, and others to express themselves. In the Architecture and Design Hall, children can build using blocks and tubes, operate a miniature crane, or play with a miniature train. It also include a large drawing table and a climbing structure with a tunnel to slide soft blocks down.

The Discovery Hall features a changing hands-on exhibit. It has included Arthur's World, a facsimile of Arthurs world that the kids could play in, and a Dr. Seuss exhibit.

The San Francisco Bay Hall allows children to explore aspects of the San Francisco Bay.

The water play area is great fun on fair-weather days and is often the highlight for children. It is outside and is like a small running stream at about the kids waist level. It is filled with water toys. They have waterproof smocks, but forget about them. Most children will walk away from here totally drenched. Save this section for last and bring a change of clothes.

Learning labs, toddler and preschooler workshops, special events and performances, art workshops and family workshops are available. This is a fabulous museum that you can never get tired of visiting. To avoid crowds, visit between 2:00 p.m. and closing.

You will be walking from barracks to barracks, so this isn't a great rainy day activity. And, for safety reasons, strollers are not allowed in the barracks. Stroller parking is available outside each building. The entire museum is double-stroller friendly. If your walkers tend to stay close to you, go ahead and brave one adult per two children. However, if your kids tend to wander, you might want to try this one adult per child. It is easy to lose sight of children due to the number of rooms at Discovery Museum.

A café is on the premises where you can grab nutritious snacks and beverages.

Hwy 101 to Alexander Avenue exit. Follow the brown and white signs to East Fort Baker and then to the Bay Area Discovery Museum.

Bay Model Visitors Center
Sausalito—2100 Bridgeway/Spring Street
(415) 332–3870 / www.spn.usace.army.mil/bmvc

Hours: Memorial Day to Labor Day—9:00 a.m. to 4:00 p.m. Tuesday through Friday, 10:00 a.m. to 5:00 p.m. Saturday and Sunday;
Labor Day to Memorial Day—9:00 a.m. to 4:00 p.m. Tuesday through Saturday

Fee: Donations appreciated

A little out of the way, this reproduction of the San Francisco Bay demonstrates tidal action and mixing of fresh water from the Sacramento River with salt water of the bay in a two-acre scaled model. The model only operates when an experiment is in progress, but the facility is filled with interactive displays and historical exhibits and photographs of the heyday of Sausalito as a shipbuilding community. This is best visited with preschoolers and older.

Food Food is available at nearby Mollie Stone's grocery store (off Bridgeway) as well as in downtown Sausalito (go one block off Bridgeway to avoid the tourist traps).

Driving Hwy 101 to the Sausalito–Marin City exit. Follow the signs to Sausalito until you are getting there towards downtown Sausalito on Bridgeway. Turn left onto Harbor, then almost immediately turn right onto Marinship Way and follow the signs to the Bay Model.

North Bay

Water Play: Beaches, Lakes, Pools & Boating

Angel Island State Park
Tiburon—Middle of San Francisco Bay
www.cal-parks.ca.gov and www.angelisland.org

Angel Island State Park is a beautiful place where families can get away from the hectic pace of San Francisco. With incomparable view of San Francisco, East Bay, and Marin Headlands, either beach—Ayala Beach or Quarry Point—are sure to please. The small, protect Ayala Beach extends across part of the cove's shore and is one of the few places around the Bay where toddlers can romp safely and relatively warmly. Beyond Ayala Cove are more than 13 miles of trails and roadways for hiking and biking. The main picnic area at Ayala Cove can be crowded, so get there early or set out on a trail that leads around or over the island and find your own private picnic spot with an incredible view. Be sure to grab a trail map, includes elevations, at the visitor center and determine what your little ones are capable of. While at the visitors' center, you can check out the display on local history and the role of Angel Island in the settlement of the west.

Food / Make a Day

During the summer month, there is a concession stand. In addition, motorized, one-hour tram tours ((415) 897–0715) will take you around the island.

Getting There

From San Francisco, Pier 41 (Blue & Gold Ferries (415) 705–5555) is a 40-minute ride—10:00 a.m. and 11:30 a.m. Monday through Friday; 9:45 a.m., 11:30 a.m., 2:00 p.m. Saturday and Sunday. Adults (13+) $10.50, Children (6-12) $5.50, Under 6 is free. Bicycles $1.00

From Tiburon (Angle Island Ferries (415) 435–2131) is a 10-minute ride—May through September Hourly 10:00 a.m. to 3:00 p.m. Monday through Friday, Hourly 10:00 a.m. to 5:00 p.m. Saturday and Sunday; April & October 10:00 a.m. to 3:00 p.m. Wednesday through Friday, 10:00 a.m. to 5:00 p.m. Saturday and Sunday; November & March 10:00 a.m. to 4:00 p.m. Hourly Saturday and Sunday; December through February 10:00 a.m. to 3:00 p.m. Saturday and Sunday. Adults (12+) $7.00, Children (5–11) $6.00 children, Under 5 is free. Bicycles $1.00.

From Oakland/Alameda (Blue & Gold Ferries (415) 705–5555) is a 70-minute ride—9:00 a.m./9:10 a.m. Saturday and Sunday. Adults (19+) $12.00, Juniors (13–18) and Seniors (62+) $9.00, Child (5–12) $6.00

Freitas Park
Seen entry in Parks & Playgrounds, review.

North Bay

McNear's Beach

San Rafael—201 Cantera Way/San Pedro Road
(415) 446-4424 / www.co.marin.ca.us

North Bay

Hours: Park—Open daily
Pool—Memorial Day to Labor Day—10:00 a.m. to 6:00 p.m. Daily

Fee: Per car $7.00
Pool—Over 3 $7.00, Under 3 free

Part of Marin County's regional park system, this 55-acre park includes a wading pool and an Olympic-sized pool in an enclosed, fenced area. The large pool is slightly cold and not especially clean, but the baby pool is slightly warmer and in the shade. There are tennis courts and a large grassy area with picnic tables (a nice place for a weekday picnic but crowded on weekends), a beach area, and a fishing pier. Children can play on the sandy beach and there's lot of room for running on the grass. No playground equipment.

Food There is a snack bar.

Driving 101 N to Central San Rafael exit. East to San Pedro Road.

Muir Beach

West Marin County on Highway 1
(415) 388-2595 /www.nps.gov/muwo

Located at the foot of Mount Tamalpais, this secluded, wind-swept beach is very peaceful. The beach is only about a mile long in a semi-circular cove. This is one of the few beaches where campfires are allowed. Dogs are also allowed, on a leash (although many dogs run free). In addition to the beach, there are hiking trails and picnic facilities. Rogue waves and undertoe currents can occur without warning, so if you choose to let your toddlers go near the water, be sure to hold their hand.

Driving Hwy 101 to CA-1/Stinson Beach exit. Drive about .5 miles. At the stoplight, turn left. Drive about 5.2 miles (passing the turn to Muir Woods) Turn left at the Pelican Inn. Continue to the beach parking lot, about 0.25 miles.

Rodeo Beach

Sausalito—Ft. Cronkhite in the Marin Headlands
(415) 331-1540 / ww.nps.gov/goga

This small beach is near the former headquarters of Ft. Cronkhite. It isn't protected as is Muir Beach, so the surf can very rough. It is great for sandy play and little ones will enjoy the pebbly beach as well as the surfers. There is access to hiking trails from the beach and National Park Service ranger-led programs.

Other facilities in the vicinity of the hostel include the Headlands Institute (environmental education), Headlands Center for the Arts, and the Marine Mammal Center (see review on topic).

101 North, first Sausalito Exit, turn left and wind your way over the hills to the former military headquarters

North Bay

Stinson Beach

Stinson Beach, Hwy 1
(415) 868-1922 / ww.nps.gov/muwo

Stinson Beach boasts three miles of beautiful white sand and surf, stretching beneath the steep hills of Mt Tamalpais with vistas from mountain to sea. Swimming is advised only from late May to mid-September when lifeguards are on duty. As anywhere near the Pacific, toddlers should be hand-held near the water. No animals are allowed on beach. The parking lot fills up quickly on warm days, so call ahead to find out about the parking situation.

Food is available in shops, grocery stores and restaurants along Hwy 1. Grab lunch and head to the Stinson Beach Village Green Playground (see review on topic) for a picnic.

Food

101 to CA-1/Stinson Beach exit. Drive about .5 miles. At the stoplight, turn left. You now have two options, both about the same distance, both on winding steep roads. Hwy 1 takes you along the ocean, Panoramic Highway take you along the shoulder of Mt. Tam. Drive about 2.7 miles. At the top of the hill, turn right onto the Panoramic Highway towards Muir Woods/Mount Tamalpais. Continue on about 12 miles to Stinson Beach. OR Continue straight on Highway 1 about 12 miles to Stinson Beach.

Driving

Swim Center

Petaluma—900 East Washington
(707) 778–4410

Hours: May through September—1:00 p.m. to 4:15 p.m. Daily

Fee: Adults $2.00, Child (6 and under) $1.00

This two-acre swim center has a 50-meter heated outdoor pool and a HUGE heated wading pool that is two-feet deep and limited to children age 5 and under. Swim diapers are allowed. The complex includes showers, dressing rooms, a large deck, grassy area and picnic areas. Swim lessons and other classes are also offered; call for more information.

There is a playground close by. Kids might find the skateboard park next door fun to watch.

Driving Hwy 101 to Washington Street exit. Head west.

North Bay

Out and About: Hikes, Bikes & Stroller Trails

Muir Woods

West Marin County on Highway 1
(415) 388–2595 / www.nps.gov/muwo

North Bay

Fee: Adult (16+) $2.00

The beautiful 560-acre National Monument offers six miles of trails, 1.5 of which are wide, flat, paved, and great for both strollers and novice walkers. Four bridges spanning Redwood Creek allow loop walks lasting 1/2 hour, 1 hour, and 1 1/2 hours, and interpretive signs and brief volunteer-led ecology walks allow manageable bites of learning. Upon arriving, go to the visitors center for a trail map and recommendations on which trails are best for your children. One adult per child is recommended for this destination because you have to keep a close watch on adventurous toddlers who can veer off main trail, climb through large gaps in the wooden fences lining the trail, or fall into the stream from any of the bridges. The park is cool, moist, and shaded most of the year, so jackets are advised. It's a perfect destination for a very hot day.

This is a very popular tourist destination, so the parking lot adjacent to the entrance fills up fast on busy weekends. Therefore, it's best to visit on weekdays, or early or late on weekend days.

Snacks and gifts are available at shops near Muir Woods Road.   **Food**

Hwy 101 N to CA-1/Stinson Beach exit. Drive about .5 miles. At the stoplight,   **Driving**
turn left. Drive about 2.7 miles. At the top of the hill, turn right towards Muir
Woods/Mount Tamalpais. Drive about 0.8 miles. At the 4-way intersection, turn left
towards Muir Woods (oncoming traffic has the right of way!). Continue down the
hill about 1.6 miles. The Muir Woods parking lot will be at the bottom of the hill,
on a sharp turn, on your right.

Tennessee Valley Beach Hike

Mill Valley—Tennessee Valley Beach

Tennessee Valley Beach Hike is about four miles round trip and gently leads downhill towards the beach and back up. The hike ends at a beautiful sandy beach with crashing waves and large rock formations. There is some shade available close to the cliffs, but bring sun hats for everyone! This hike is a perfect outing to soak up the sun, see nature, and expend some energy. The hike is double-stroller friendly—about one-third of the hike is on asphalted surface and not a problem for any stroller size, while the rest is on well-trampled paths that are wide enough for two double strollers. The last 200 yards are sandy and you will need to park stroller.

Food There is a fruit stand with snacks at the turn-off from Highway 1, but it is best to bring your own snacks and food or picnic. Tamalpais Junction, part of Mill Valley, is a five-minute drive from the trailhead.

Hwy 101 to Stinson Beach/Mill Valley exit, drive underneath bridge, watch for signs for first country road to the left labeled "Tennessee Valley"; follow road about 3 miles until it ends in big parking lot. Be advised that on weekends you might have to park on the side of the road)

West Point Inn
Mill Valley—Mt Tamalpais
(415) 388–9955

The West Point Inn is one of a number of inns that rose to serve Marin's now defunct train network. The rustic building is located about two miles from the Pan Toll trailhead and is accessible by the Stage Coach Road, a trail that is wide enough and flat enough to be used by jogging strollers or young walkers.

The Inn offers special pancake breakfasts once a month in the summer (Mother's Day, Father's Day, and one Sunday a month in July, August, September, and October) from 9:00 a.m. to 1:00 p.m. It also offers lemonade and candy for purchase.

Driving 101 to Stinson Beach Exit, take Hwy 1 to Panoramic Hwy to Pan Toll trailhead

North Bay

Trains, Planes & Automobiles

Napa Valley Wine Train
Napa—1275 McKinstry Street
(800) 427-4124 / www.winetrain.com

North Bay

Hours: Brunch—8:20 a.m. to 11:30 a.m. Weekends; Lunch—10:00 a.m. to 2:30 p.m.
Weekdays, 10:00 a.m. to 3:30 p.m. Weekends; Dinner—4:00 p.m. to 9:30 p.m.
Weedays, 3:30 p.m. to 9:00 p.m. Weekends

Entrance Fee: Brunch—$59.50 per peson, Lunch—$70.00 per person; Dinner—$79.00
per person; Prices do not include wine. Children (12 and under) can order from
the brunch, lunch, or dinner menu for $22.50

Experience gourmet dining aboard restored 1915 Pullman dining and
lounge cars while gently gliding past picturesque vineyards of Napa
Valley. This is really for families with preschoolers and older or those
with extremely well-behaved younger children. Once you are on the
train, you are there for the next 2.5 to 3 hours.

29 N to Lincoln Avenue exit. East on Lincoln Avenue. Right onto Soscol Avenue.   **Driving**
Left onto First Street. Immediate Left onto McKinstry Street.

Traintown
Sonoma—20264 Broadway St.
(707) 938-3912 / www.traintown.com

Hours: Memorial Day through Labor Day—10:00 a.m. to 5:00 p.m. Daily; Labor Day
through Memorial Day—10:00 a.m. to 5:00 p.m. Fridays through Saturday and
Holidays. Closed Thanksgiving Day and Christmas Day

Fees: Train Fare—Adults $3.75, Seniors and Children (16 months–16) $3.25.
Rides—$1.75 per ticket or $10.00 for eight-ticket book

Traintown is a 10-acre railroad park filled with replicas of animals, natural
features, historic buildings, and structures. Fifteen-inch gauge live-steam
locomotives and diesel replicas pull long passenger trains through the
park, stopping at a petting zoo along the way. Passengers will go over
bridges and trestles, as well as through tunnels. There are some full-sized
equipment available for viewing. Traintown also includes several rides,
such as a restored Ferris wheel, merry-go-round, and carousel. Although
Traintown is fairly stroller accessible, this activity is best for children
who are walking.

Food   There is a snack bar at Traintown. The square in downtown Sonoma is a great place to bring a picnic or grab a pizza at Mary's Pizza and/or or ice cream next door.

Driving   CA-37 E towards Napa/Vallejo. Bear left on Arnold Drive towards Napa/Sonoma. Right onto Fremont Drive. Continue on Broadway Street.

North Bay

Peninsula

A baby is born with a need to be
loved and never outgrows it.

Frank A. Clark

Parks & Playgrounds

Bayside Park/Joinville Swim Center

San Mateo—Kehoe Avenue
(650) 522–7400 / www.ci.sanmateo.ca.us

This playground is between the Bayside Park and the Joinville Swim Center. It has one large climbing structure with great slides and is underlain by wood chips. It's best for the preschooler and older.

Driving   101 S to Third Avenue exit. East on Third Avenue. Right onto Norfolk. Left onto Kehoe.

Beresford Park

San Mateo—28th Street/Alameda de las Pulges
(650) 522–7400 / www.ci.sanmateo.ca.us

Beresford Park contains one small play structure for toddlers and one larger structure for children ages 3 to 6, as well as lots of things for older children to climb on, around, and in. Only the toddler area is fenced.

There is also a recreation center that has programs for children from 9 months to 5 years—check San Mateo's activities guide for more information. Beresford Park also has a large grassy area with picnic tables, basketball courts, and tennis courts.

Food   Food can be obtained nearby on El Camino.

Driving   101 S to 92 W. Exit Alameda de Las Pulgas. Left onto Alameda de Las Pulgas.

Burton Park

San Carlos—Cedar Street/Arroyo Avenue
(650) 802–4382 / www.ci.san-carlos.ca.us

This park was voted the best park in the Bay Area by readers of Bay Parents Magazine. It includes two play structures underlain by wood chips and sand. One, a fenced-in playground, is appropriate for toddlers. The second, a larger playground with new equipment, is best for older children (ages 3 to 6). Both playgrounds have picnic tables that can be reserved.

Burton is the main park of the city of San Carlos and, as such, offers many services. There is a large grassy area as well as baseball diamond,

Peninsula

basketball courts, tennis courts, soccer field, and recreation center. **Food**
Snacks and food can be obtained nearby on El Camino. **Driving**
101 S to Brittan exit. Southwest on Brittan. Right onto Cedar Street.

Central Park
San Mateo—5th Street/El Camino Real
(650) 522–7400 / www.ci.sanmateo.ca.us

This large park has tennis courts, a botanical garden, Japanese tea garden, baseball field, large grassy area, recreation center, and playground. The playground has both wooden play structures for toddlers and an older children's climbing structure. It also has a sit-on backhoe and older metal playground equipment, as well as infant and regular swings. Although the playground is not fenced, the entire park is fenced so children can't wander too far. A small ride-on train (see description elsewhere) on a circular track is 75¢ per child and runs on Saturdays, Sundays, and holidays. A snack bar is in the park and sells hot dogs, pizza, and soft drinks. You can wander through the Japanese tea garden.
3rd Street in San Mateo has many eateries, including a North Beach pizza.
A great independent toy store, Talbots Toyland, is located on 4th Street.
101 S to 3rd Avenue exit. East on 3rd Avenue. Left on El Camino Real.

Peninsula

Commodore Park
San Bruno—Cherry Avenue/Commodore Drive
(650) 616–7180 / www.ci.sanbruno.ca.us

The four-acre park has two playground structures. The newer one is brightly colored with four slides, various climbing structures, a truck dashboard with steering wheel, and two rocking animals. All are on a rubberized flooring. The posted recommendation for the structure is for ages 5 to 12, but parts of the structure would be appropriate for toddlers if they are not wanderers. The structures are not enclosed and that particular structure is adjacent to the street. The older part of the playground has sand, swings, a merry-go-round and an old wooden structure for big kids. There is a large grassy area and plenty of big trees for shade. The paved walkway throughout the park is perfect for tricycles. There is a softball field and several picnic tables with bbq grills. **Food**
Bayhill Shopping Center is a quarter mile further south on Cherry Avenue and contains a supermarket, drug store, and several eateries.
280 S to Sneath/San Bruno Avenue exit. East on Sneath. Right onto Cherry Avenue

Coyote Point Recreation Area
San Mateo—Coyote Point Drive
(650) 363–4020 / www.eparks.net

Fee: Parking $4.00

This playground was the first to conform to California's regulations mandating disabled-friendly playgrounds. As such, this one includes an extra wide slide (so parents can ride with their kids), a rubberized mat surface (to soften landings), harnesses for swings (to hold children who cannot sit independently), and wheelchair ramps, as well as instructions in Braille and an olfactory garden.

The playground is also unusual in that it was built by 300 orthopedic surgeons in partnership with Kaboom, an organization dedicated to building safe playgrounds (www.kaboom.org); United Cerebral Palsy; and San Mateo County Department of Parks and Recreation.

Coyote Point Recreation Area includes a marina, a beach area, a segment of the San Francisco Bay Trail, and the Coyote Point Museum for Environmental Education. It is also one of the best windsurfing locations in California.

This recreation area includes plenty of picnic tables. Food can be found at the restaurant located in the recreation area, or you can bring your own.

Hwy 101 S to Poplar Ave. exit. Right onto Humbolt. Right onto Peninsula

Cuernavaca Park
Burlingame—3075 Hunt Drive/Alcazar Drive
(650) 558–7330 / www.burlingame.org

If you're looking for a place for a quick stop to re-energize restless kids after a long drive along 280, this is a good option. This park features three older metal play structures suitable for preschoolers and older. Infant swings and older children swings are also available. There is a basketball court adjacent to the playground which can also be used for roller skating or trike riding. This playground is out of the fog bank and the weather is usually sunny, affording visitors great views of the Bay and the airplanes landing at SFO. However, it can get windy in the afternoons and be sure to bring your sunscreen because there is no shade.

Food   The closest commercial area is at the bottom of Trousdale Drive (down the hill at El Camino REal). Here you'll find the Plaza shopping center with a Lombardi's grocery strong, Sees candy, and coffee shop.

Driving   Hwy 280 to Trousdale exit

Peninsula

Frontierland Park

Pacifica—Oddstad Boulevard/Yosemite Drive
(650) 738-7380

This is perhaps the best new playground in the Bay Area. ' is set in a pocket of hills above the City of Pacifica (and the usu fog layer) and enjoys a lovely view of the surrounding mountains. The original playground (a very rustic old wooden structure geared to older children) and basketball court still exist, but are now encircled by a huge field of grass, a group picnic area with cooking facility (for use by reservation) and a brand new playground opened in 2002. The playground structure is a product of the same company who manufactured San Anselmo's Millenium Park playground, and the play area is divided into two sections -- one for the younger set (2-5) and older kids (5 and up). Kids can choose from a variety of climbing structures complete with towers, hanging bridges, chimes, climbing walls, water misting feature, balance beams, dozens of slides, sand box, swings -- it is hard to think of any feature that is missing. It takes a while to drive to Frontierland Park, but it is totally worth a visit, and be prepared to spend several hours. Bring a picnic lunch to eat on the field. After you're done at the playground, you can easily stop at the beach (Pacifica State Beach - Coast Highway at Linda Mar Boulevard) on the way home or at the huge bowling alley on the east side of the Coast Highway as you drive north back to San Francisco. Hwy 280 to CA-1 towards Pacifica. Left onto Fassler Avenue. Right onto Terra Nova Boulevard. Left onto Oddstand Boulevard. Right onto Yosemite Drive.

Peninsula

Gull Park

Foster City—Gull Avenue between Killdeer Court/Swan Street
(650) 286-3380 / www.fostercity.org

Gull Park has all the delights of the beach without the hassles. It is generally sunny and the water is warmer than the ocean. There are no waves, the water is still like a lake (but it is salty). The water is roped off at about waist level to keep kids contained. You can roll your double stroller right up to the sand and unload. The park is great for plane sightings and there are three play structures to appeal to various ages. A big grassy area can be a soccer or frizbee field and the trees around it make shade on the hot days. If you want exercise, the peninsula trail is nearby and is adjacent to the Bay. North, under the San Mateo bridge (92) goes to Coyote Point (see review) and south will take you clear to Redwood City. Hwy 101 to Hillsdale exit. East on Hillsdale. Right onto Gull Avenue

Make a Day

Highlands Recreation Center
San Mateo—1851 Lexington Avenue
(650) 341–4251 (Pool) / www.highlandsrec.com

Hours: Pool—Recreation swim hours vary. See web site.

Fees: Pool—$5.00 San Mateo Resident; $10.00 Non-Resident

Highlands Recreation Center packs a lot of activity options into a small space. It includes a playground, tennis courts, swimming pool, and fitness center. The play structure is a newer metal structure set upon wood chips and is located at the base of the parking lot. The swimming pool and fitness center are located further up the hill. The swimming pool includes both a lap pool and a kiddie pool. During the summer, it is an outdoor pool and, when the weather changes, a dome is placed on it to make it an indoor pool. Swim diapers are required for those 4 and under. In addition, swim lessons are provided for those 3 and older.

Hwy 280 S to CA-35/Bunker Hill Dr/Half Moon Bay exit. Left onto Skyline Boulevard. Left onto Bunker Hill Drive. Right onto Lexington Avenue.

"J" Lot
Burlingame—Primrose/Burlingame Avenue
(650) 558–7330 / www.burlingame.org

After a stroll up and down Burlingame Avenue, the upscale shopping street, your children are likely to be a big figidty in their stroller. Head towards the J Lot playground and let them work some of that energy off. The fenced play area is in the corner of the parking lot on Primrose Street.

After some play time, why not reward your children's patience with a treat from Copenhagen Bakery and Café (1216 Burlingame Avenue) or walk two blocks north on Primrose to Bellevue and peruse the large collection of books and puzzles at the Burlingame Public Library.

Hwy 101 S to Broadway exit. Continue on Broadway. Left on El Camino Real. Left on Burlingame Avenue.

Lakeshore Park
San Mateo—Norfolk Street/Marina Court
(650) 522–7480 / www.ci.sanmateo.ca.us

Peninsula

Food / Make a Day

Driving

Lakeshore Park includes one large play structure underlain by sand and wood chips for children ages 2 to 6. There is also a lagoon with beach area where kids can play with water. Park also has a recreation center, as well as a basketball court and softball field.

Hwy 101 S to Hillsdale Boulevard exit. East on Hillsdale. Left onto Norfolk Street. **Driving**
Right onto Marina Court

Parkside Aquatic Park and Beach

San Mateo—Roberta Drive/Seal
(650) 522-7400 / www.ci.sanmateo.ca.us

Parkside Aquatic Park is perfect for introducing your younger ones to open waters. The warm temperatures, lack of current, and roped off swim area will allow you to relax just a little while your children splash in the water. The swim area graduates from a sandy beach to about four feet. Pedal boats and sailboats can be rented. The park also includes one play structure underlain by sand that is appropriate for children ages 1.5 to 4.

If you don't pack enough snacks, they sell goodies at the snack shop.

Hwy 101 S to Third Avenue Exit. East on Third. Right onto Norfolk Street. Left onto Roberta Drive. Right onto Seal.

San Bruno City Park

San Bruno—1300 Crystal Springs Ave/Oak Avenue
(650) 616-7180 / www.ci.sanbruno.ca.us

This huge park has tennis courts, a baseball diamond, an outdoor swimming pool, two playgrounds, a snack bar, picnic tables, and a large grassy area. The largest playground, located near Lara Field, has two sections. One section is devoted to toddlers and the other to school-aged children. The toddler area has a merry-go-round with little horses, a ride-on dinosaur, two backhoes, a play structure with several slides, and baby swings. The school-age section has a tall climbing structure with several slides, swings, tire tubes, and merry-go-round. There are picnic areas for rental and many birthdays parties occur on the weekends. The picnic area near the large playground has a stream and bridge that create a nice atmosphere. The smaller playground, located near the tennis courts, has a small play structure and benches for parents to sit.

The snack bar is open on most weekends. And, El Camino Real is a few **Food**
blocks east with many eateries.

I-380 to CA-82 exit towards El Camino Real/San Bruno. Left onto El Camino Real. **Driving**
Right on Crystal Springs Avenue.

Peninsula

Stafford Park

Redwood City—King Street/Hopkins Avenue
(650) 780-7250 / www.redwoodcity.org

This park can get crowded, but that is because it is such a great park. The playground is quite large and nicely separates the older kids from the younger kids. There are numerous slides and forts for kids to enjoy on either side. When the weather turns warm, a very popular fountain is turned on so kids can run through it and cool off. This playground is worth a long drive from San Francisco—check out pictures of it on the web site.

Driving Hwy 101 S to Whipple exit. Right onto Whipple. Left onto Lowell.

Village Park

Burlingame—1535 California Avenue/Rosedale
(650) 697–3598 / www.burlingame.org

This is a neighborhood park that is large but not very well used. The playground has three play structures located at the rear corner of the park, all in sturdy primary-color plastic, underlain with wood chips. One toddler structure has two slides and steering wheel; the other two preschool structures have a high slide, bridges, and swinging areas. There is a sandbox, two dinosaur built-in ride-ons, and swings. There are five shaded picnic tables, basketball courts (great for riding tricycles), and a large grassy area (partially shaded). The park is fenced except for one small entrance area. Easy access to the recreation center and its equipment.

This is the home of the Village Park Preschool so it can get crowded during weekdays. Weekends are the spot for many birthday parties (first come, first serve). But it's always sunny and clean, especially when San Francisco is fogged out.

Food It's located in a residential neighborhood but eateries on Broadway Avenue are just a short drive away.

Driving Hwy 101 S to Broadway/Burlingame exit. West on Broadway. Right onto California

Peninsula

Washington Park

Burlingame—850 Burlingame Avenue
(650) 558-7300 / www.burlingame.org

The playground in Washington Park has three plastic play structures, one geared to toddlers with slides and swings. The other structures have slides, bridges, tire swings, and climbing areas. There's a water play area and the children will have a lot of fun playing with the water and making sand castles. Be sure to bring a change of clothing for your kids. Keep in mind that the playground area is shaded in the morning but does get hot during the afternoon. Washington Park is a great all-purpose park consisting of the playground, as well as a baseball field, basketball courts, tennis courts, picnic grounds, a large grassy area, and a rose garden.

Burlingame Avenue is located across the tracks from the playground with many local eateries including Noah's Bagels, sandwich shops, and Starbucks. The park has numerous benches and tables for picnic lunches.

Food

The Burlingame Train Station is only three short blocks away, which is an enjoyable way to spend an afternoon. For $4.50, an adult and two children can ride to California Station in Palo Alto and visit another playground on the east side of the station, then return home. Free musical concerts at Washington Park are offered at 1:00 p.m. on Sundays in July. Burlingame Aquatic Center is located next door at 400 Carolan Avenue (see description elsewhere).

Hwy 101 South to Broadway/Burlingame exit. West on Broadway. Left onto Carolan. Left onto Burlingame Avenue.

Peninsula

Animals: Zoos, Farms & Nature Centers

Coyote Point Museum for Environmental Education
San Mateo—1651 Coyote Point Drive
(650) 342–7755 / www.coyoteptmuseum.org

Hours: 10:00 a.m. to 5:00 p.m. Tuesday through Saturday
12:00 p.m. to 5:00 p.m. Sunday

Fees: Adults (18+) $6.00, Seniors & Youth (13 – 17) $4.00, Child (3-12)
$2.00, Under 3 and San Francisco Zoo members are free.
Free first Wednesday of each month.
Vehicle fee $4.00

This is the Bay Area's only environmental science museum and is best for the preschooler and older. The focus of the museum is the Environmental Hall composed of exhibits featuring the six major ecosystems found in the Bay Area. The exhibits are separated by a wonderful double-stroller-friendly elevated ramp which

Little ones will love the exhibits.

youngsters love to run and gallop on. The museum also houses several gardens, including a new kids garden, hummingbird garden, and a butterfly garden. Children will revel in the cave-like, glass enclosed atmosphere of the Wildlife Habitats Center, which houses live reptiles, amphibians, mammals (coyotes, etc.) and birds. There is a river otter feeding at 12:15 p.m. daily and a fox feeding at 11:30 a.m. daily. Weekend animal talks are held at 2:00 p.m. Saturday and Sunday. You might need more than one adult to visit the museum depending on how well your children stay close.

Family membership to the Coyote Point Museum will also give you entry to the San Francisco Zoo, Chabot Observatory, and Lawrence Hall of Science.

Food Coyote Point Recreation Area has a high-end restaurant, but it might be easier to bring your own food and have lunch in the picnic grounds.

Make a Day Coyote Point Recreation Area includes hiking trails, boat launches, and a salt marsh. It also has a great playground for little ones. There's a nice trail along the water's edge which is a great place to watch airplanes land/take-off at SFO. You can enjoy a nice picnic lunch while you watch planes land.

Driving Hwy 101 S to Poplar Ave. exit. Right onto Humboldt. Right onto Peninsula Avenue.

Peninsula

Fitzgerald Marine Reserve

Moss Beach—Moss Beach off Hwy 1
(650) 728-3584 / www.eparks.net

If your kids like the tide pool area at the Academy of Sciences, they will enjoy seeing the real thing in one of the most diverse areas in the state to view tide pools. This 30-acre reserve protects over 200 species of animals and 150 species of plants. Kids will love looking at snails, starfish, hermit crabs, sea anemone, and coral. Be sure you go during low tide (call the Marine Preserve to find out). Bring non-slip shoes for everyone and be prepared to walk down a steep, but small, dirt hill to reach the beach.

The parking lot has picnic tables as well as a small, one-room visitor center. If you're lucky, a volunteer naturalist will be out at the tide pools answering questions.

Driving Hwy 1 to California Street in Moss Beach. West. Fitzgerald Marine Reserve is at the end of the street.

Hidden Villa Farm and Wilderness Preserve

Los Altos Hills—26870 Moody Road
(650) 949-8650 / www.hiddenvilla.org

Peninsula

Hours: 9:00 a.m. to dusk Tuesday through Sunday
Closed to the public for its Summer Camp Program during the summer.

Fee: $5.00 parking fee

Founded in 1925 by Frank and Josephine Duveneck, this 1,600-acre wilderness preserve offers an organic garden and a working farm with animals such as cows, sheep, pigs, chickens, goats, and rabbits. Take a self-guided tour of the farm or call to reserve a spot on one of their hour-long guided tours (11:00 a.m. to 1:00 p.m. Sunday, $5.00 per person, kids under 2 free). After seeing the farm, consider taking a hike—the area has miles of trails. September through May, Hidden Villa has workshops and classes in environmental education as well as the arts and humanities.

Driving Hwy 280 to El Monte/Moody Road exit at Foothill College in Los Altos. Left onto Moody Road

Lemos Family Farm
Half Moon Bay—12320 San Mateo Rd
(650) 726–2342

Hours: 9:00 a.m. to 5:00 p.m.Saturdays and Sundays 9:00 a.m. to 5:00 p.m.
9:00 a.m. to 5:00 p.m.Weekdays around Halloween and Christmas

Fee Day Pass —Child $15.00, Adult $5.00
Individual Prices—Pony rides and play area $4.00, Train $2.50, Petting Zoo $1.00

Lemos Farms has something for all those who are walking—pony rides, petting zoo with goats and aggressive sheep, bounce house and play structure, snack bar, tractor train, picnic tables, grass area, and a creek flowing throughout. The farm can be rented for birthdays so it can be crowded on weekends. Ponies are very docile and well-behaved. Only the play area, petting zoo and pony ride areas are fenced. Cowboy-themed songs play from loudspeaker ("Happy trails to you …").
During Halloween, they have great selection of pumpkins (at expensive prices). Christmas trees offered over Christmas holidays.
There is a winery, trout farm, and nurseries west on Highway 92. Tide pools available at Fitzgerald Marine Reserve on Highway 1 in Half Moon Bay; fun for kids of all ages. The Pillar Point Harbor has many great seafood restaurants or you can buy fresh fish just off the boat at the harbor. Weather can be unpredictable so bring a sweater and sunscreen.
Hwy 280 S to Hwy 92 W to San Mateo Road

Palo Alto Junior Museum and Zoo
Palo Alto—1451 Middlefield Road
(650) 329–2111 / www.pajmzfriends.org

Hours: 10:00 a.m. to 5:00 p.m. Tuesday through Saturday
1:00 p.m. to 4:00 p.m. Sunday
Closed holidays

Fee: Donations appreciated

Created in 1941, this educational museum is home to the PlaySpot (with safe, stimulating exhibits designed for children under five), and Zoo (including animals from the local habitat such as raccoons, bobcat, bats, geese, hedgehog, snakes, crows, and owls). The PlaySpot includes an area to make your own movies (Foley voiceovers), stop-motion filmmaking, videography, an art room and clay room. On Saturdays, the Bay Area Reptile Society displays their snakes, lizards, frogs and other amphibians that can be handled and displayed in a non-threatening environment. The Museum offers workshops, camps and birthday parties for those interested.

Hwy 101 to Embarcadero exit. Right onto Middlefield Road   Driving

Peninsula

Water Play: Beaches, Lakes, Pools & Boating

Brisbane Community Swimming Pool
Brisbane—2 Solano Street at Mariposa
(415) 657–4321 / www.ci.brisbane.ca.us

Hours: Contact. Varies by season.

Fees: Non-residents—Adults (18+) $4.00, Child (Up to 17) $2.25
Annual pass Adult $40.00, Child $35.00

Brisbane Community Pool is a great family-oriented facility located close to San Francisco. It has a toddler pool and a lap pool offering zero-depth entry for easy disabled access that is also great for kids. Family Swim hours allow use of flotation devices and water toys in the lap pool. Swim lessons begin at 1 year. The best time to visit this swim complex is on a very hot day, as the location can get extremely windy and uncomfortable.

Surrounding the pool is a grassy area and a shaded structure with picnic tables. Vending machines provide the usual (candy, soda, and ice cream).

A playground with climbing equipment, swings, and plenty of sand is located next door to the pool facility.

Hwy 101 to Brisbane/Cow Palace exit. Right on Bay Shore Boulevard. Right on Old County Road. Right on Mariposa. Right on Solano.

Burlingame Aquatic Center
Burlingame—400 Carolan Ave/Oak Grove.
(650) 558–7322 / www.burlingame.org

Hours: May through September. Contact for recreational swim hours.

Fees: Adult $3.00, Child (2–17) $2.00, Under 2 are free

The complex, built in 2000, has an Olympic-sized pool and a great kiddie pool. Both are heated between 78 and 82 degrees year-round and handicapped-equipped. Swim diapers for kids are required. There are lap swim times, but also recreational swim times that stretch multiple hours in the afternoons.

There is a wonderful playground located in Washington Park (see review), next door to the Aquatic Center. Only three short blocks away is the Burlingame Train Station. Taking the train to Burlingame

Peninsula

Park adds to the fun.

Burlingame Avenue is also located across the tracks from the playground with many local eateries including Noah's Bagels, sandwich shops, and Starbucks.

Food

Hwy 101 S to Broadway/Burlingame exit. West on Broadway. Left on Carolan

Driving

Rinconada Pool and Park Complex
Palo Alto—**777** Embarcadero Road at Middlefield Road
(650) 463–4914 / www.city.palo-alto.ca.us

Hours: May through September. Contact for recreational swim times.

Fee: Adult $3.00 weekdays, $4.00 weekends; Youth $2.00 weekdays, $3.00 weekends; Under 3 free

Rinconada Park is home to a terrific playground, a great pool complex, and the wonderful Palo Alto Junior Museum and Zoo (see review). The pool complex includes a large Olympic-sized lap pool and a clover-shaped wading pool that is 2 feet and less in depth. The wading pool (heated to approximately 80 degrees) has four lifeguards and includes a water slide, fountains, and ride-on motorcycles which squirt water.Swim lessons are available during the summer starting at age 3. There is a lawn area and shaded section next to the wading pool, but there are no in and out privileges. The park has two large play structures (Adventure Ship and a water play area), a fenced-in totlot, and a huge, grassy lawn area. Tennis courts and bbq pits are available.

There isn't a snack bar in the park, but many restaurants are located in downtown Palo Alto, on El Camino Real, and in Stanford Shopping Center.

Hwy 101 to Embarcadero exit

Driving

Peninsula

Rockaway Beach
Pacifica—Rockaway Beach/Pacifica Plaza and Beach

This is a nice, short outing even for those with very young children. If you are just interested in looking at waves, soaking up some sun, and making a short but successful little trip out of the house, this is the one you should try. Even at 1.5 years, children can run around on the plaza, collect rocks, build little rock piles, and have lunch in the sun. You can either stay on the asphalted plaza or make your way onto the beach area. Surfers hang out near this location and the kids love to look at them.

Hwy 280 to Hwy 1 to Pacifica. Rockaway Beach exit.

Driving

San Bruno City Pool

San Bruno—1300 Crystal Springs Ave/Oak Avenue
(650) 616–7191 / www.ci.sanbruno.ca.us

Hours: May through September. Contact for recreational swim times.

The San Bruno City Pool is located within the very large San Bruno City Park (see review). It includes a large pool, as well as a toddler pool. The toddler pool is two-feet-deep and heated to a warm 83 degrees. Swim lessons begin at 4 years of age. However, there is a program for infants 6 months and their caregivers.

Driving I-380 to CA-82 exit towards El Camino Real/San Bruno. Left onto El Camino Real. Right on Crystal Springs Avenue.

San Gregorio State Beach

San Gregorio—Hwy 1
www.parks.ca.gov

This is a gorgeous beach with white sand surrounded by high rock cliffs that even the most agile climber will not be able to scale. A small stream cuts across the beach making it a great place for little ones to swim and play safely without worrying about a rogue wave knocking them over.

Driving About 1 hour south of San Francisco, but definitely worth a day trip. The beach adjoins Hwy 1, just south of the Hwy. 84/La Honda Road

Peninsula

Other Outside Activities

Filoli Historical House & Gardens

Woodside—86 Canada Road
(650) 364–8300 / www.filoli.org

Hours: Mid-February through October—10:00 a.m. to 3:30 p.m. Tuesday through
Saturday

Fees: Adult $10.00, Students $5.00, Children (7–12) $1.00, Under 7 are free.

Filoli Gardens is a great place for taking your stroller-bound babies and
getting you out of the house on a sunny day. Located in the warm
Peninsula, it is often delightful when it is foggy in San Francisco. There
is a charming café for lunch, and a fountain that lulls babies to sleep while
you eat. After lunch, you can steer your stroller through the 16-acres
of incredible gardens. You'll have to do some exploring to find the
ramped paths and avoid the stairs, but the volunteers, mostly retired,
will help you out and coo over your babies. There are lovely benches
throughout the gardens. Strollers are allowed in the Filoli Historical
House if you want to look around. Filoli Gardens offers an Easter Egg
Hunt, Mother's Day Brunch, and Holiday Traditions if you're looking
for some old-fashioned, genteel fun.

Hwy 280 to Edgewood Road exit. Right onto Edgewood Road until it dead ends at
Canada Road. Right onto Canada Road.

Peninsula

Trains, Planes & Automobiles

Hiller Aviation Museum

San Carlos—601 Skyway Road
(650) 654–0200 / www.hiller.org

Hours: 10:00 a.m. to 5:00 p.m. Daily

Fees: Adults $8.00, Youth (8–17) $5.00, Under age 8 free with paying adult

Dedicated to the dreams of flight since June 1988, the museum highlights many historic flight-related advancements native to Northern California (e.g. the Stanford wind tunnel) and shows how technologies resident here today will shape the future of air transportation. Your child—2.5 years and older—will love sitting in an interactive UH-12 helicopter and pretending to fly, climb in the cockpit of a Blue Angel and working the gears, and observing the Star Wars Phantom Menace pod planes with Sony PlayStation simulated flight. Young children are sure to enjoy the observation area on the second floor that offers a direct view of the flight pad of the San Carlos Airport, with audio from the radio tower. Small commuter planes arrive and depart nearly every minute from this busy airport.

The second floor also contains a Bay Area Airline historical collection, videos about careers in aviation, and a pictorial on pioneer women in aviation. The Atrium in the lobby contains the gift shop (one of the largest collections of aviation toys, books, flight wear, models and memorabilia), restoration shop (allows visitors to witness the ongoing restoration process through its large picture windows), Children's Area (featuring puzzles, Duplo blocks, a play airstrip and Stealth Bomber play planes, and ride-on airplanes) and theater (visitors sit on actual airplane seats to watch a video about the birth of aviation). The Main Gallery houses over forty vintage and futuristic aircraft in life-sized proportions, prototypes, photographic displays, and models in a large hanger.   In the rear of the museum, between the main gallery and the San Carlos Airport, nose sections of Boeing's 747 and 737 commercial airplanes and a Compass Rose may be viewed.

Food   There are coin-operated snack and drink machines in museum. The Burger King next door has airplanes hanging from the ceiling and a helicopter in front which children can sit in and pump the pedals. There's also a more upscale Houlihan's Restaurant next door that offers a variety of California cuisine favorites.

Driving   Hwy 101 S to Holly Street/Redwood Shores Pkwy. exit. East onto Redwood Shores Pkwy. Right onto Airport Road. Right onto Skyway Road.

Peninsula

Miniature Train
San Mateo—5th Street/El Camino Real
(650) 340–1520 / www.ci.sanmateo.ca.us

Hours: 10:30 a.m. to 12:45 p.m. Weekdays
11:00 a.m. to 3:00 p.m. Weekends

Fee $1.00 per person

This is a private concession since 1976 is located in Central Park. It's just a miniature train that goes around in a circle. Parents can ride in it but it's a tight squeeze. A project room and the train can be rented for special occasions.
101 S to 3rd Avenue exit. East on 3rd Avenue. Left on El Camino Real.   **Driving**

Peninsula

South Bay

Kids: they dance before they learn there is
anything that isn't music.

William Stafford

Parks & Playgrounds

Bachman Park

Los Gatos—401 Bachman Avenue/Belmont Street
(408) 399–5770 / www.town.los-gatos.ca.us

Bachman Park is a small neighborhood park located a few short blocks from Santa Cruz Avenue, site of old town Los Gatos' charming shopping district. The park is across the street from a row of restored bungalow-style homes and enjoys a view of the Santa Cruz mountains—making it one of the more scenic spots in the area. The play structure is small but relatively new and swings are available for infants and big kids.

Benches and picnic tables are scattered throughout the park (the playground is surrounded by a large expanse of lawn and dotted with several mature trees) making it the perfect place to kick back with a burrito from Andale (on Santa Cruz Avenue) and enjoy Los Gatos' perfect summer weather.

Driving CA-17 S to CA-9 exit towards Los Gatos/Saratoga/Monte Sereno. Left onto Massol Avenue. Right onto Bachman Avenue.

Doerr Park

San Jose—Potrero and Park Wilshire
(408) 794–1383 / www.sjparks.org

This is a nice, small park in a quiet neighborhood. It is partially fenced and includes an interactive/hands-on play structure with a train, store, and musical pipes. The main play structure is very new and made of metal and plastic. There are some little rocking planes and two infant swings. Everything is underlain by rubber matting or wood chips. This is a popular destination on Friday mornings, but is otherwise not heavily used. Older kids structures are a short distance away and are of the older metal variety with a high slide.

Driving Hwy 280 to Meridian exit, go west until Curtner, turn right; left on Dunbarton, right on Potrero

South Bay

McEnery Park

San Jose—San Fernando Street
(408) 277-5904 / www.grpg.org,

McEnery Park, part of the Guadalupe River Park & Gardens, has something for kids of all ages, including a number of structures that are quite unique. There is a fenced playground that includes a climbing structure as well as spring toys and a model boat. The highlight, however, is the area some kids refer to as spider web park, a large area of plastic nets and ropes fashioned into a climbing structures that look like th Eiffel Tower, London Bridge, and other famous landmarks. If you have good climbers over 3, you have to let they try this unusual play space! McEnery Park also includes a small-scale Guadalupe River, perfect for sand and water play. Your kids will absolutely love this place whether they like running and climbing everywhere or sitting quietly building a sand castle.

Other parts of Guadalupe River Park & Gardens (see review) include Tot Lots (see review), Carousel (see review), and Children's Discovery Museum (see review)

Driving Hwy 87 S to Park Avenue exit. Left onto Park Avenue. Right onto Woz Way. Or, Hwy 87 N to San Carlos Street exit. Right onto San Carlos Street. Right onto Woz Way.

Memorial Park

Cupertino—Mary Avenue and Stevens Creek Boulevard
(408) 777–3120 / www.cupertino.org

This lovely 28-acre park includes fields of green grass, a large duck pond, meandering creek, and a brand new children's play area. The multiple climbing structures are made of metal and plastic, have lots of levels and slide tubes to explore, and are surrounded by shaded picnic tables. The play area is underlain by sand. Infant swings and regular swings are next to the climbing structures. A separate, small toddler structure is across the park. The beautiful new Quinlan Community Center is also nearby. Memorial Park also includes an amphitheater, a softball field, and tennis courts.

Food Shopping centers abound along Stevens Creek Boulevard. Whole Foods Market is a few blocks further down Stevens Creek Boulevard.

Driving Hwy 85 to Stevens Creek Blvd exit. Left over freeway. Left onto Mary Avenue. Parking lot is behind Senior Center.

South Bay

(walking to about 2 years) and includes baby swings and a toddler-size play structure with a slide. The second area has a couple of slides and lots of climbing structure for older kids. Both are underlain with tanbark. There are two softball diamonds—children might love to watch the softball leagues practice—and a pair of tennis courts. There are also several picnic tables throughout the park and lots of grassy area. This is a neighborhood park and there are usually young children playing here.

The recreation center holds various programs, including gymnastics. The gymnastics classes are taught by Twisters gymnastics and are very popular.

Food There is a small deli and convenience store on Foothill Boulevard about half a mile past the park. There is also a Whole Foods Market with a large deli/prepared food section on Stevens Creek Boulevard a couple of miles from the park.

Driving Hwy 280 to Foothill Blvd. exit. Head up the hill and park will be on your right just after the Stevens Creek Blvd. intersection. Or, Hwy 85 to Stevens Creek Blvd. exit. Left onto Foothill Blvd.

Serra Park

Sunnyvale—739 The Dalles Ave. between Hollenbeck/Lewiston Avenues
(408) 730-7350 / www.ci.sunnyvale.ca.us

Serra Park has a play area with slides and climbing structures (sand underlayment) that is good for confident walkers though the sand is nice for all ages. There is a second play area with a mock river boat and a water play area. The park also has a man-made creek and lots of open grass area.

There is a nice paved walkway that goes past the river boat play area and several features on the creek.

There is a PW Grocery store with a deli on Homestead Avenue about a mile from the park. There are also several small stores and restaurants in the strip malls on the corners of Homestead and Hollenbeck Avenues.

Driving CA-85 S to CA-82 S. Exit El Camino Real/Sunnyvale. Continue on El Camino Real. Right onto Hollenbeck Avenue. Right onto The Dalles Avenue.

South Bay

Tot Lot

San Jose—Highway 880 in the north to Hughway 280 along the Guadalupe River
(408) 277-5904 / www.grpg.org,

The Guadalupe River Park & Gardens offers a host of activities for everyone. The Tot Lot playground includes a climbing structure and fort, as well as slides, swings, and a climbing pyramid. The most unique attraction, however, is a fabulous collection of one-of-a-kind net and rope climbing structures located near the Carousel. Good climbers (age 3 and above) will delight in the challenge of scaling a tower, a dome, and a bridge made entirely of rope.

Other parts of Guadalupe River Park & Gardens (see review) include **Make a Day** McEnery Park (see review), Carousel (see review), and Children's Discovery Museum (see review).

Hwy 87 S to Park Avenue exit. Left onto Park Avenue. Right onto Woz Way. **Driving** Or, Hwy 87 N to San Carlos Street exit. Right onto San Carlos Street. Right onto Woz Way.

Vasona Lake County Park

Los Gatos—Blossom Hill Road
(408) 356–2729/www.parkhere.org

Vasona is the jewel in the crown of the Santa Clara parks. The area includes a beautiful lake, a 151-acre park, and the Los Gatos Creek Parkway. The park and adjacent parkway have many different activities, including hiking, fishing, paddleboats (Boat Rentals (408) 972–1188 during the spring and summer), a model boat pond, and a wonderful playground for children of all ages.

Miniature train rides on the Billy Jones Wildcat Railroad (see review) start in Los Gatos' Oak Meadow Park and run through Vasona Park.

Oldtown in Los Gatos (50 University Avenue) has many restored **Food** buildings with Spanish and Victorian architecture, intermingled with gardens, shops and restaurants.

Hwy 17 S to Lark Avenue exit. Go east. Right onto Los Gatos Blvd. Right onto **Driving** Blossom Hill Rd. Entrances are located on Garden Hill Drive and University Avenue

South Bay

Animals: Zoos, Farms & Nature Centers

Happy Hollow Park and Zoo
San Jose—1300 Senter Road in Kelley Park
(408) 277–3000/www.happyhollowparkandzoo.org

Hours: July 6 through August 25—10:00 a.m. to 5:00 p.m. Monday through Friday
10:00 a.m. to 6:00 p.m. Saturday and Sunday
Remainder of Year—10:00 a.m. to 5:00 p.m. Daily
Closed Christmas Day

Fee: Ages 2-64 $5.00, Under 2 and over 75 are free
2nd Tuesday of month $1.00
Parking fee of $5.00

This park is geared to children aged 2-10, and that age group loves it— especially the primary-colored rides and the close proximity of the animals in the zoo. The park includes rides such as Danny the Dragon Train, Bug Ride, King Neptune's Carousel, Crooked House slide, maze play area, remote-controlled boats, mirror house, treehouse, as well as daily puppet shows. There are several play areas scattered throughout the ride area including one with backhoes and ride-on dinosaurs, one with modern plastic play structure, and a few older, metal-barred climbing structures.

The zoo houses over 150 animals of 50 species, including jaguars, hedgehogs, monkeys, miniature horses, rabbits, lemurs, pygmy hippos, miniature pigs, reptiles, and birds. The lemur exhibit is especially engaging with the popularity of PBS' Zoboomafoo and with two new babies born in the May 2001. There is a large petting zoo with goats and rabbits. It is best to come during the week as it is less crowded

A large grassy area near the Crooked House is great for picnics, and the Riverboat Wharf and Viking Ship have picnic tables. The Kid's

Food Café is located in the ride area, and includes french fries, burgers, and other favorites.

Make a Day Kelley Park has large grass areas, playgrounds, and bbq area. The Kelley Park Express Train, a steam train which pulls two bench-platformed open air cars to the San Jose Historical Museum, runs every 45 minutes on weekends and costs $1.50.

Driving Hwy 101 to Story Road west exit. Left onto Senter Road. Or, Hwy 280 to 10th Street south exit. Left onto Keyes. Right onto Senter Road.

South Bay

Museums: Art, Science & Hands-on

Children's Discovery Museum

San Jose—180 Woz Way at Auzerais Street
(408) 298-5437 / www.cdm.org

Hours: 10:00 a.m. to 5:00 p.m. Tuesday through Saturday
12:00 p.m. to 5:00 p.m. Sunday

Fees: Ages 1–59 $7.00, Senior (60+) $6.00, Under 1 is free

The museum is housed in a vast (52,000 sq. ft) purple building, filled with exhibits that stimulate creativity and learning through hands-on exploration. Exhibits cover facets of science/technology, music, art, history, and community relations and are great for preschoolers and older. This museum is well-endowed and hosts numerous excellent traveling exhibits as well as ones developed with the support of Silicon Valley businesses. The museum is a favorite destination for school field trips, so Friday mornings are particularly busy. The Museum also offers classes for children (starting at age 2) and their caregivers.

Food The Kids' Café (pizza, etc.) is located within the museum, and just across the street is Guadalupe River Park & Gardens which is nice for picnic lunches. A number of fast-food and family-type restaurants are located nearby in downtown San Jose.

Combine a trip to Children's Discovery Museum with any of the other activities located within the Guadalupe Rive Park & Gardens area (see review).

Hwy 280 S to Bird Avenue exit. Left onto Bird. Right onto Auzerais Street. Right onto Woz Way. The nearest parking is in a city-owned lot on Woz Way (daily rate varies from $3.00-$7.00).

South Bay

Other Outside Activities

Guadalupe River Park & Gardens

San Jose—Along the Guadalupe River
(408) 277-5904, (408) 999–6817 Carousel / www.grpg.org,

Hours: Park & Gardens—Sunrise to Sunset Daily
Visitor Center—11:00 a.m. to 5:00 p.m. Thursday through Monday
Carousel—May 1 to Labor Day 10:00 a.m. to 7:00 p.m. Monday through
Sunday Labor Day to Fall 10:00 a.m. to 5:00 p.m. Tuesday through Sunday
Winter 11:00 a.m. to 5:00 p.m. Tuesday through Sunday

Fees: Park & Gardens—Free
Visitors Center—Free
Carousel –$1.00 per ride
Children 12 and under ride free second Tuesday of month

Guadalupe River Park and Gardens is a three-mile work-in-progress (completion projected at the end of 2004) and offers something for everyone including playgrounds, picnic areas, hiking and biking paths by the river, extensive public gardens, a 930-square-feet Monopoly Board, and a Visitor Center and Ranger Station. It is divided into four sections: (1) Arena Green; (2) Gardens; (3) Discovery Meadow; and (4) McEnery Park.

Arena Green is across from the San Jose Arena (Autumn/Santa Clara streets) and includes many attractions for kids of all ages. There is a carousel that includes six fiberglass animals custom-made for San Jose— two sharks representing San Jose's famous ice hockey team, a hummingbird, coyote, salmon, and eagle—as well as 27 other traditional carousel animals. The Ranger Station and Visitors Center is also in the Arena Green area and include exhibits on indigenous plants and animals as well as maps, brochures, educational programs (such as docent-led garden and park tours, plant and garden workshops, and a Water Wizard Day Camp for children ages 7 to 10), and other information. The Tot Lot (see review) is also located in this area.

The Gardens include four different gardens for strolling. The Discovery Meadow is home to the Children's Discovery Museum (see p. ___) and the location for large festivals. And, McEnery Park is entirely focused on a child's experience (see review).

Food Food is located at a small concession stand near the carousel and in the downtown area just a few blocks south.

Driving Hwy 87 S to Park Avenue exit. Left onto Park Avenue. Right onto Woz Way.
Or, Hwy 87 N to San Carlos Street exit. Right onto San Carlos Street. Right onto Woz Way.

South Bay

Los Troncos/Monte Bello Open Space Preserves

Santa Cruz Mountains—Page Mill Road/Skyline Boulevard
(650) 691-1200 / www.openspace.org

Both the Los Troncos and Monte Bello Open Space Preserves are great for kids who like to hike. Both showcase lots of earthquake features, and Monte Bello sports an abandoned orchard and a sag pond, an earthquake fault-induced lake. In the Los Troncos preserve, children can walk the very popular San Andreas Fault Trail. It is a 1.5 mile trail with numbered markers that correspond to the brochure you can pick up in the parking lot and enable you to see a variety of San Andreas Fault features. On a clear day you can see all the way to San Francisco to the north and Mt. Ummanum to the south.

Food

There are no picnic tables but plenty of nice spots to stop for a picnic. There are great views from the hill above the parking lot, a very short walk up the trail.

Driving

The preserve's entrance is on Page Mill Road, 7 miles west of Highway 280 and 1 mile east of Skyline Boulevard. Parking is available for 20 vehicles. Additional parking and restroom facilities are available at the Monte Bello Open Space Preserve parking area, directly across Page Mill Road.

Stevens Creek County Park

Cupertino—11401 Stevens Canyon Rd.
(408) 867-3654 / www.parkhere.org

Fees: Per car $4.00, Annual county park pass $50.00

This is a good park for kids who are confident walkers, and a good place to start introducing your kids to *wilder* parks. There are remnants of orchards, lots of native plants and a variety of wildlife (hawks, deer, lizards). This park is best for jogging strollers though there is a paved area and hard-packed dirt paths that are okay for small-wheel strollers near the first entrance. For your construction-minded kids there is a good view on weekdays of the working quarry (bulldozers, dump trucks, and lots of big gravel trucks) from the lakeside picnic area.

Food

There are a variety of picnic areas in the park. You can pick up food at the small deli and convenience store on Foothill Blvd. about three quarters of a mile from the first park entrance. There is also a Whole Foods Market with a large deli/prepared food section on Stevens Creek Blvd. about four miles from the park.

Driving

Hwy 280 to Foothill Blvd. exit. Cross Stevens Creek Blvd. intersection. Or, Hwy 85 to Stevens Creek Blvd. exit. Left onto Foothill Blvd.

South Bay

Trains, Planes & Automobiles

Billy Jones Wildcat Railroad
Los Gatos—Oak Meadow Park
(408) 395-7433 / www.bjwrr.org

Hours: March 15 through June 14—10:30 a.m. to 4:30 p.m. Weekends
June 14 through Labor Day—10:30 a.m. to 4:30 p.m. Daily
Day after Labor Day through October 31—10:30 a.m. to 4:30 p.m. Weekends
November 1 through March 14—11:00 a.m. to 3:00 p.m. Weekends
Carousel is open during train hours plus additional hours. Check the web site.

Fee: Train $1.00, Under 2 are free

Take a ride on a one-mile, eight-minute loop through Oak Meadow Park. You'll cross a 40-ft wooden trestle and an 86-ft long bridge over Los Gatos Creek, as well as see a hand-operated turntable. A 1910 Savage carousel is next to the railroad station, as well as playground structures, picnic areas, paddleboats, and duck pond.

Driving Hwy 17 S to Lark Avenue exit. Right onto Lark Avenue. Left onto University. Left onto Blossom Hill Road.

Kelley Park Express Train
San Jose—Happy Hollow Park & Zoo, 1300 Senter Road in Kelley Park
(408) 277-3000/www.happyhollowparkandzoo.org

Hours: 12:00 p.m. to 5:00 p.m. Tuesday through Sunday
Closed Thanksgiving, Christmas and New Year's Day

Fee: $1.50, Parking $5.00

This steam train pulls two bench-platformed open air cars between the San Jose Historical Museum and the Happy Hollow Zoo. Unfortunately, it's not terribly reliable so plan your trip around the other activities in the area. And, if you get lucky, you might be able to take a ride.

Driving Hwy 101 to Story Road west exit. Left onto Senter Road. Or, Hwy 280 to 10th Street south exit. Left onto Keyes. Right onto Senter Road.

South Bay

Danny the Dragon Train

San Jose—1300 Senter Road in Kelley Park
(408) 277–3000/www.happyhollowparkandzoo.org

Hours: See Operating Hours for the Happy Hollow Park and Zoo
Danny the Dragon Train runs on weekends when zoo is open

Fee: $1.75 plus admission to the Happy Hollow Zoo

Happy Hollow Zoo (review) has a variety of rides for young children, including Danny the Dragon. This small train seems to magically glide along a path through the zoo. Danny was built in 1960 and is the last remaining of four dragon trains.

Driving   Hwy 101 to Story Road west exit. Left onto Senter Road. Or, Hwy 280 to 10th Street south exit. Left onto Keyes. Right onto Senter Road.

Roaring Camp & Big Trees Narrow Gauge Railroad

Felton—Graham Hill Road between Hwy 17 and Hwy 9
(831) 335–4484 / www.roaringcamprr.com

Hours: April through October, Daily
November through March, Weekends

Fees: Adults (13+) $15.50, Child (3-12) $10.50, Under 3 free
Season Pass $50.00
Parking $5.00

Antique steam locomotives take passengers on a 6.5 mile round trip (about an hour) through the redwoods. The trains are located in a recreated old-time logging camp complete with 1880s general store, operating sawmill, and chuckwagon bbq. There are special events on many holiday weekends, such as Memorial Day, July 4th, Labor Day, Halloween, Thanksgiving, and Christmas.
The Santa Cruz Big Trees and Pacific Railway departs from the same depot (see description below).

Driving   Hwy 17 to Mt Herman Road exit. Right onto Mt Herman Rd. Left onto Graham Hill Rd.

South Bay

Santa Cruz Big Trees and Pacific Railway

Felton—Graham Hill Road between Hwy 17 and Hwy 9
(831) 335–4484 / www.roaringcamprr.com

Hours: May 12 through June 14, Weekends and Holidays
June 15 through September 2, Daily
September 7 through October 27, Weekends and Holidays
December, Special Holiday Trains

Fees: Adults (13+) $17.00, Child (3-12) $12.00, Under 3 free
Season Pass $60.00
Parking $5.00

Passengers can board a beach train and travel to Santa Cruz along the route that was used by picnickers in 1875. This three-hour roundtrip will take you through the Henry Cowell Redwoods State Park and over the spectacular San Lorenzo River Gorge, all the way to the Santa Cruz Beach Boardwalk.

The Roaring Camp & Big Trees Narrow Gauge Railroad departs from the same depot (see description above).

Driving Hwy 17 to Mt Herman Road exit. Right onto Mt Herman Rd. Left onto Graham

South Bay

Index

Aquariums
See also Tide Pools

Beaches

Index

Biking

Boats/Boat Rentals

Bowling

Carousels

Index

Index

Hiking

Index

Index

Parks and Playgrounds

Index

Index

Index

Index

Index

Stroller Walks

Swimming
See Beaches, Lakes, Pools

Tide Pools

Trains

Index

Wildlife Centers

Zoos
See also Petting Zoos

Worth a Drive Over a Bridge

- Central Park (San Ramon) East Bay
- Habitot Children's Museum (Berkeley) East Bay
- Contra Loma Reservoir (Antioch) East Bay
- Children's Fairyland (Oakland) East Bay
- Bay Area Discovery Museum (Sausalito) North Bay
- Frontierland (Pacifica) Peninsula
- McEnery Park (San Jose) South Bay
- Moscone Playground (Marina) San Francisco

MUST SEE Playgrounds

- Central Park (San Ramon) East Bay
- Howarth Park (Santa Rosa) North Bay
- Millennium Playground (San Anselmo) North Bay
- Gull Park (Foster City) Peninsula
- Moscone Playground (Marina) San Francisco
- Children's Playground (Golden Gate Park) San Francisco

Great for the Stroller-Bound or Crawlers

- South Beach Children's Play Area (China Basin) San Francisco
- Habitot Children's Museum (Berkeley) East Bay
- Baby Brigade (Oakland) East Bay
- Strybing Arboretum & Botanical Gardens
- Filoli Historical House & Gardens
- California Academy of Sciences

San Francisco is an amazing town for young musicians. There are great outdoor places to listen and play. My favorite is at the Marina, where there is a giant wind organ at the end of the pier. Also try Golden Gate Park in the field next to the Carousel, where there are always great drummers jamming in the sun. They love for the little ones to come and dance to the music, and to try and beat out a few tunes on the drums.

Paul Godwin
Director of Music Together of SF
www.musictogethersf.com

If there were no schools to take the children away from home part of the time, the insane asylums would be filled with mothers.

Edgar W. Howe

It is with great pleasure that we present to you one of the most useful outing guides that young parents can ever have. It has been so useful to my family and friends that we just had to publish the 3rd Edition. Enjoy!

A.K. Crump
Publisher
TCB-Café Publishing
www.cafeandre.com